ALLEN CARR'S EASY WAY TO QUIT EMOTIONAL DRINKING

SIRIUS

*To **Ian McLellan**, a hero of our publishing exploits for more than 25 years in 50 countries worldwide, and to **Cris Hay** and **Tim Glynne-Jones** for their amazing contribution in making this book happen.*

SIRIUS

This edition published in 2024 by Arcturus Publishing Limited
26/27 Bickels Yard, 151–153 Bermondsey Street,
London SE1 3HA

Copyright © 2023 Allen Carr's Easyway (International) Limited

ISBN: 978-1-3988-1470-7
AD010593US

Printed in the UK

ALLEN CARR

Allen Carr was a chain-smoker for over 30 years. In 1983, after countless failed attempts to quit, he went from 100 cigarettes a day to zero without suffering withdrawal pangs, without using willpower, and without putting on weight. He realized that he had discovered what the world had been waiting for—the easy way to stop smoking—and embarked on a mission to help cure the world's smokers.

As a result of the phenomenal success of his method, he gained an international reputation as the world's leading expert on stopping smoking and his network of centers now spans the globe. His first book, *Allen Carr's Easy Way to Stop Smoking*, has sold more than 14 million copies, remains a global bestseller, and has been published in over forty different languages. Hundreds of thousands of smokers have successfully quit at Allen Carr's Easyway centers where, with a success rate of over 90 percent, they guarantee you'll find it easy to stop or your money back.

Since 2020 the World Health Organization has been using Allen Carr's Easyway method to assist its quit smoking programs across the globe and, in 2022, the UK Government's National Institute for Health & Care Excellence issued guidance recommending that NHS/Local Authority Smoking Cessation Services should make this method available to smokers contacting them for help.

Allen Carr's Easyway method has been successfully applied to a host of issues, including alcohol, sleep, weight control, and other addictions and fears. A list of Allen Carr centers is on page 226. Should you require any assistance or if you have any questions, please do not hesitate to contact your nearest center.

For more information about Allen Carr's Easyway, please visit **www.allencarr.com**

Allen Carr's Easyway

The key that will set you free

CONTENTS

IT'S ESSENTIAL THAT YOU DON'T SKIP THIS IMPORTANT
INTRODUCTION

BY JOHN DICEY, GLOBAL CEO AND SENIOR THERAPIST, ALLEN CARR'S EASYWAY

Allen Carr's reputation in the field of addiction treatment and behavior change was built on his huge success in helping smokers to quit. His Easyway method was so successful that it quickly became, and remains, a global phenomenon. From the earliest days of Easyway, Allen was inundated with requests from sufferers of countless other addictions and issues, imploring him to help them. By the turn of the century, he had assembled a team of highly skilled, loyal, and dedicated senior therapists who went on to help him not only apply his method to a variety of addictions and issues, but also play a key role in delivering Allen Carr's Easyway method across the world.

The responsibility for ensuring that all our books are faithful to Allen Carr's original method is mine, and it's an honor to be writing this important introduction. Rest assured, once you've read it, I'll leave you in Allen's capable hands. It has been suggested to me that I describe myself as the author of the books we've published since Allen passed away. In my view, that would be quite wrong.

That's because every new book is written strictly in accordance with Allen Carr's brilliant Easyway method. We have merely updated the format to make it as relevant as possible for the modern-day audience. There is not a word in our books that Allen didn't write or wouldn't have written if he were still with us and, for that reason, the updates, anecdotes, and analogies that are not his own—that were contemporized or added by me—are written in Allen's voice to seamlessly complement the original text and method.

I consider myself extremely privileged to have worked closely with Allen on Easyway books while he was still alive, gaining insight into how the method could be applied to a growing list of issues and addictions, and together we explored and mapped out its future evolution. I was more than happy to have the responsibility of continuing this vital mission placed on my shoulders by Allen himself. It's a responsibility I accepted with humility, and one I take extremely seriously.

WHAT ARE OUR CREDENTIALS?

We've been successfully treating behavioral issues and addictions all over the world with phenomenal success over the past 39 years. Easyway's senior team and I were inspired to join Allen's quest for one simple reason: his method saved our lives. Like every Allen Carr's Easyway therapist in the world, we were all drawn to get involved with Easyway as a result of being set free from our own addictions.

Allen reveled in helping people deal with a whole variety of addictions and behavioral issues, and many of those who were lucky enough to be helped were so inspired and grateful to him, they contacted him to offer their help to advance the method. It proved to be a fertile field from which to recruit, and it was a pleasure to work with Allen in assembling the most remarkable senior therapist team to set about the task of applying the method to as many issues as possible.

The varied background of behavioral issues and drug-taking history of Allen's senior therapist team, far from deterring Allen from recruiting them, encouraged him to do so. If he was impressed by your drive, enthusiasm, ability and accomplishments, he considered it a superb bonus if you had previously experienced the misery of other issues to which Easyway could be applied. He was acutely aware that it would be extremely difficult to apply his method to the full range of behavioral issues and addictions without the direct involvement of people who had experienced them first-hand. Whether weight or eating issues, fear of flying, gambling, debt, heroin, cocaine, cannabis, alcohol or nicotine addiction—direct, up close, and personal experience of those issues enabled Allen and his team to develop the method accordingly.

This book is the direct result of our determination to apply Allen's brilliant method as far and as wide as possible, and I'm delighted that we have finally provided the solution for anyone whose life has been blighted by emotional drinking. And we've done so with confidence. How can we do that?

SIMPLE: THIS METHOD WORKS!

Our motivation for putting the method down in writing was to enable anyone, anywhere in the world, regardless of wealth, to benefit from *Allen Carr's Easy Way to Quit Emotional Drinking*. This book cannot replicate what we do at our Live Group Seminars, which are led by experienced Allen Carr's Easyway therapists/ facilitators who present this method in a dynamic, interactive way—with plenty of opportunities to address questions or concerns as they arise and which also include telephone/email support, and free of charge, back-up sessions for the few that require them. The seminars are so successful that we offer a money-back guarantee.

Make no mistake, this book is a highly effective, complete program in itself and, after our Online Video Programme, it is the very next best thing to attending a Live Group Seminar. Perhaps that statement might dishearten you somewhat—but please do not allow it to—Allen Carr's Easyway books have led tens of millions of people to freedom and everything you need in order to become one of them is in your hands right now.

I'm aware that many people who are unfamiliar with the method, or who have never met people who have benefited from Easyway, assume that some of the claims made about it are far-fetched or exaggerated. That was certainly my reaction when I first heard them. I was incredibly fortunate to have had my life saved by Allen Carr. There is no doubt that had my addiction not brought me into contact with Allen and his amazing method in the late 1990s, I would not have made it to the 21st Century—let alone be here today!

I'm incredibly proud to have headed up the team which, over the past 25 years, has taken Allen's method from Berlin to Bogotá, from New Zealand to New York, from Sydney to Santiago and beyond.

I still take pleasure in deflecting all the praise and acclaim straight back to the great man himself: it's all down to Allen Carr.

The method is as pure, as bright, as adaptable, and as effective as it's ever been, allowing us to apply it to a whole host of addictions and issues. Whether it's alcohol, smoking, sleep, cannabis, cocaine, heroin, sugar addiction, gambling, junk spending, fear of flying, practicing mindfulness, or even digital/social-media addiction, the method guides those who need help in a simple, relatable, and plain-speaking way.

Please don't mistake Allen Carr's Easyway method for some kind of "Jack of all trades." As you're about to discover, there is no doubt that it truly is the master of all behavioral issues and addictions.

Now, without further delay, let me pass you into the safest of hands—Allen Carr and his "Easyway."

Chapter 1

THE KEY

Do you drink to help you cope with difficult emotions? Do you feel trapped by alcohol? Do you find yourself helpless to resist the temptation of a drink, even when you're alone? Do you sense that you perhaps drink a little too much, a little too often? If so, you've become trapped in the miserable prison of emotional drinking, and it's time to escape. The good news is, you're holding the key.

Emotional drinking is a disorder that involves the use of alcohol in an attempt to relieve uncomfortable emotions, such as anxiety, stress, loneliness, and boredom. Most people have experienced the compulsion to use "Dutch courage" when facing a daunting situation, or a "stiff drink" to calm them after a trauma. But that compulsion can make you a slave, turning your life into a destructive cycle of drinking, guilt, misery… and more drinking.

MY CLAIM

This book has been written to help people who have found themselves caught up in this vicious circle of drinking, guilt, and misery. It addresses the mental process that leads to emotional drinking and tackles it head on.

Reading this book will help you understand what's going on in your mind, and why, and then to change your mindset so that you no longer have the desire to drink for comfort.

Unlike other methods for controlling drinking, you won't have to make any sacrifices. Nor will you have to draw on your willpower to overcome the temptation to drink or battle a feeling of deprivation. Furthermore, you will find that, having escaped from the prison of emotional drinking, you won't be susceptible to falling back into it.

Right now you may consider this claim too good to be true. The conventional wisdom tells us that issues like emotional drinking are powerful and complex and require immense willpower to overcome. This book will explain why this is misguided. In fact, it is fundamentally unhelpful, actually working against your efforts to cure yourself.

The truth is that you can easily stop drinking in response to your emotions without any pain, sacrifice, or willpower. This applies regardless of who you are and what your personal circumstances may be. All you need is an open mind.

If you're skeptical about that, ask yourself one question: has conventional wisdom worked for you? If it had, you wouldn't feel the need to read this book.

ADDICTION

Alcohol is an addictive drug, but many emotional drinkers balk at accepting that they are addicted. They know they need help to quit, but they reject the term "alcoholic."

The common conception of an alcoholic is a sloppy drunk, disheveled, reeking of booze, and incapable of lucid thought or conversation. These people are nothing like that—in fact, in most cases they are functional and conceal their drinking problem incredibly well.

Why do they conceal it? Because society is utterly intolerant of alcoholics. Addiction is seen as a weakness, something to be ashamed of rather than a condition that warrants sympathy and understanding. Society's attitude toward alcohol is full of contradictions. While other addictive drugs are marginalized, alcohol is embraced as not only socially acceptable but a social necessity. Try throwing a party without booze!

As soon as we are old enough to drink legally in public (and often before), adults take great joy in buying us our first alcoholic drinks, encouraging us to push through those first repulsive sips and "develop a taste for it." And then they laugh knowingly when we overdo it and get sick, and when it comes to celebrating life's finer moments, how do they go about it? With Champagne!

But when the woman next door starts smelling of booze; when you see her smashed at one party after another; when she fails to show up at school to pick up her kids; how does society react? With tutting, shakes of the head, and whispers about how she could be so irresponsible.

The point being that society is wholly intolerant of alcoholics. It is assumed that the problem is of their own making—they are weak in some way, or self-indulgent. Somehow they have failed to control their drinking. It's no wonder, then, that anyone with a drinking problem does their utmost to hide it. This only makes the problem worse. In hiding it from society, we also hide it from ourselves. In other words, we deny that we have a problem and thereby deny ourselves the opportunity to solve it.

Let's get one thing straight: addiction to alcohol is not a weakness. It is something that can happen to anyone—strong- or weak-willed, rich, poor, short, tall, highly educated, or highly ignorant. The reason society thinks it's a weakness is because we are all fooled into believing we control our alcohol intake. The opposite is true: anyone who drinks is controlled by alcohol.

"Alcoholic" is not a word or label we use at Easyway. It is steeped in decades of misinformation, misunderstanding, and stigma. The most powerful hindrance of all is the assertion that alcoholism is an incurable, lifelong disease which leaves those who suffer with it facing two choices:

1. Carry on drinking and suffer the consequences;

2. Stop drinking and face a lifetime of misery, deprivation, or struggle… every day until they die.

I have only good news for you—there is another way. You can get free without any shame, misery, deprivation, or struggle, and without feeling that you have a lifelong disease that can never be cured. That third way is called Easyway and all you need to do is carry on reading and follow the instructions.

Can you acknowledge that you have a problem with alcohol? There's no shame in that. Around seventy percent of adults are controlled by alcohol; it's just that most of them don't realize it or want to admit it.

Once someone is addicted to a drug, part of the brain known as the "reward pathways" are corrupted. Reward pathways are triggered by naturally occurring hormones to make us feel good when we do something that is healthy or beneficial, thus encouraging us to keep doing it. Drugs such as alcohol also trigger the reward pathways when we take them to alleviate the withdrawal or cravings that addiction causes, which is why we begin to regard them as a source of pleasure. But addictive drugs and addictive behaviors don't just corrupt the reward pathways, they bombard them, overloading them to the extent that they become dysfunctional. Eventually, the reward pathways are so numbed by this bombardment that the drug has to be taken in bigger and bigger doses for any of the phony pleasure to register, and genuine pleasures no longer register at all unless accompanied by the drug.

Happiness, sadness, stress, or relaxation are accompanied by a restless, empty feeling. In addiction terms, we call this withdrawal. When you drink again, this restless feeling is partially relieved. The effect is to make you think you've given yourself a boost. Now your brain remembers that drinking alcohol gave you a boost and is fooled into regarding alcohol as a source of pleasure and relief. So when you experience withdrawal from alcohol again, and the restless feeling returns, your brain triggers cravings for more. The fact that alcohol caused the withdrawal pangs in the first place goes unnoticed. It's the most cunning of confidence tricks.

At best, drinking to remove the discomfort of withdrawal just makes you feel closer to normal again. In other words, you have the next drink to make you feel like someone who doesn't drink at all.

Addiction is an ingenious process. It twists reality and traps the addict in a tangle of illusions. But when you see through the illusions—as you will—it all becomes incredibly clear. I'll come back to the perceived pleasures and benefits of alcohol shortly. At this stage though, it is useful for you to understand the basis of addiction—just in principle—even if you don't believe that you are addicted.

Some chronic emotional drinkers admit to deriving no pleasure from drinking, but feel powerless to stop. This despite all the sickness, guilt, and self-loathing it causes. It is one of the many paradoxes of addiction: an activity seeming to relieve emotional suffering ends up causing more of it.

The problem starts small, apparently under control, but quickly grows to take over and destroy your life. You find yourself drinking more and more, searching for satisfaction that becomes ever more elusive. Feeling unable to stop drinking, despite knowing the physical and mental harm it's causing you, is a telltale sign of addiction.

With all addictions, the cunning illusion that the drug or behavior provides a genuine pleasure or crutch is what keeps you trapped. Emotional drinkers harbor the illusion that alcohol helps them relax. In fact, as I'll explain later, it does the opposite. But the illusion of pleasure remains.

It's a vicious circle, and the longer you keep harboring the illusion that alcohol gives you pleasure or a crutch, the more miserable you become when you attempt to cut down or stop.

THE ONLY WAY TO QUIT

The term "emotional drinking" implies that there is an underlying emotional problem that drives you to drink. It could be stress, depression, fear, heartbreak, feelings of worthlessness, loneliness, boredom... or a combination of these emotions. Whatever the cause, you won't arrive at the solution through drinking.

You've probably figured that out—but you still can't seem to escape. The temptation to drink whenever you feel an emotional need is too great. It's as if you're being pinned down by a powerful monster.

The purpose of this book is to help you kill that monster and escape from the soul-destroying, repetitive cycle of emotional drinking. Free from the tyranny of that monster, you can deal with your emotions with a clear mind.

If the solution is as simple as I claim it is, you might be wondering why you haven't been able to see it for yourself. That monster is quite ingenious. It wraps you up in confusion, but the truth is incredibly simple:

THE ONLY WAY TO QUIT AN ADDICTION IS TO STOP DOING IT.

Of course, there is more to Easyway than knowing this simple truth, but it's much more straightforward than other methods, which lose sight of the obvious: the only way to quit an addiction is to stop doing it. It's *how* you go about stopping that matters. There is nothing unusual about drinking for comfort. From a young age, we are led to believe that alcohol can make you brave when you're frightened, relaxed when you're tense, confident when you're nervous, happy when you're sad, and so on.

It's only when you find yourself caught in the cycle of emotional drinking that you sense what nonsense that is. When you start drinking alcohol, you believe you're in control. You know it's not *good* for you, as such, but you believe that as long as you keep it in moderation, it won't be a problem.

And there probably would be no harm if you *were* in control. You would be able to stop whenever you wanted to. But that is not the case, is it? The compulsion to drink grows, moderation goes out the window, and helplessness, guilt, and self-loathing flood in.

It's obvious that it's not the drink itself that keeps you drinking; there's something else, like an unseen force compelling you to do it. A monster. It's the same for all addictions. You don't control the drug; the drug controls you. And the more you drink, the more you lose control.

It's safe to assume from the fact that you're reading this book that you do not feel in control. Perhaps you've tried to address the problem in the past and found you couldn't. No matter how hard you tried, you lacked the willpower. Now you drink even when you don't want to, and you believe that you're powerless to stop.

This book will show you two very important truths:

*YOU ARE **NOT** POWERLESS AND YOU DO **NOT** LACK WILLPOWER.*

The reason you have failed to overcome emotional drinking until now is simply because you were following the wrong method.

NO MORE SECRETS

Nobody likes to admit they've lost control. We regard self-control as a cornerstone of civilized behavior. It goes hand in hand with morality, dignity, and courtesy. Loss of control causes feelings of shame, and thus problems like addiction and emotional drinking are swept under the carpet. The person with the problem denies it; the rest try to avoid it.

KEEPING IT ALL TO YOURSELF CREATES A BURDEN THAT ONLY MAKES IT HARDER TO ESCAPE FROM THE TRAP.

This is no way to tackle a problem. It makes you feel very alone and compels you to try to conceal it—from others and from yourself. Secretive behavior creates feelings of guilt and shame, which deepen your misery. The first essential when tackling a problem like drinking is to acknowledge that you have it—or that it has you. The fact that you have picked up this book is a good sign that you've made that vital step.

The solution is in your hands. More accurately, it's in your mind. You need to break the cycle of misery and comfort drinking. As you read this book, be honest about your drinking and be prepared to open your mind to some truths that may seem hard to accept.

You are not alone—far from it. Emotional drinking is a global problem, threatening the health and happiness of millions, if not billions, of people. As you open your mind to the truths contained in the book, this will become obvious to you.

It will also become apparent that your problem is not caused by some flaw in your personality. The more you allow yourself to open up and unravel these myths, the more you will understand that you can conquer your addiction. And you can do so without using willpower.

THIS METHOD WORKS

Easyway is a tried-and-tested way of escaping from addictive traps like emotional drinking. It is built on the realization that addiction hijacks our instincts, so that the "fix" we turn to for relief is actually the "poison" that caused our problem in the first place.

That was the revelation that triggered this method. I was a confirmed nicotine addict, choking my way through 60 to 100 cigarettes a day and resigned to a premature death. I was under the misapprehension that smoking was a habit I had acquired and lacked the willpower to kick. The moment of revelation came when I realized that smoking wasn't a habit—it was an addiction. In that moment I saw with extraordinary clarity that my inability to quit smoking was neither a weakness in my character nor some magical quality in the cigarette. It was the trap of addiction, fooling me into seeking relief in the very thing that was causing my misery.

This led to two indisputable conclusions:

• Smoking provides no genuine pleasure or comfort.

• Therefore, stopping involves no sacrifice or deprivation.

I quit right then and there, and never felt the temptation to smoke again.

I gave the method its name, Easyway, because it required no willpower, no substitutes, and no gimmicks. It simply enabled smokers to become happy non-smokers by unraveling the brainwashing that convinced them that smoking was a pleasure or a comfort. Whether you smoke or not, I'm sure you might find that hard to believe! "Smokers don't enjoy it? Why would they risk all the downsides if they don't get anything out of it?" It takes as little as five hours to understand how the confidence trick works so let's not get ahead of ourselves here.

The method is hugely successful in helping smokers all around the world to quit. Once they remove the illusion that they are making a sacrifice by stopping, they find it easy to quit because they don't feel deprived and they are happy to be free.

I realized that this method would work for all addictions, and went on to apply it successfully to alcohol, other drugs, and even "drugless" addictions such as gambling and technology addiction.

The key was that all addictions are mainly a condition of the mind. The difficulty in stopping is around 1 percent physical and 99 percent psychological.

Easyway unravels the misconceptions that drive you to do something that does you harm, in the belief that it will give you pleasure. This applies to drinking, just as it does to any other addiction or compulsive behavior.

WHAT THIS BOOK WILL DO FOR YOU

- Change the way you think about alcohol;

- Change the way you feel about quitting alcohol;

- Show you how to quit emotional drinking immediately, easily, and painlessly;

- Enable you to enjoy genuine pleasures without drinking;

- Help you take control of your life again.

It comes with several assurances: you won't be talked down to; you won't be subjected to scare tactics or gimmicks; you won't feel deprived; and, by the end, you won't miss drinking.

By explaining how the addiction works and providing simple instructions to help you become free, this book will completely change your attitude to alcohol and show you how to enjoy a healthier, happier life. It will address the feeling of panic that can set in and cloud your judgment when trying to quit. It will help you replace deceit, guilt, and shame with openness, honesty, and confidence; it will help you take control when you feel helpless; and it will replace misery with happiness.

Many addicts feel a little miserable when they decide to quit. That's because they're full of dread. There's no need for you to be miserable or afraid. This should be a time of great excitement and joy. You're not "giving up" anything. You will not miss or yearn for anything. You will not feel there is a hole in your life, that you are missing out on something at times of stress, relaxation, joy, or sadness. On the contrary, your life will feel more complete, more balanced, and more relaxed. Isn't that something to smile about?

THE INSTRUCTIONS

As you read the book, you will come across a series of instructions. If you miss one of these instructions or fail to follow any of them, the method will not work. If you try to skip ahead and read the book in a different order than that in which it was written, the method will not work. Easyway is the key to freeing yourself from the trap you're in, and it works like the combination to a safe: if you don't use the numbers in the correct order, the safe won't open. This brings us nicely to the:

FIRST INSTRUCTION: FOLLOW ALL THE INSTRUCTIONS.

Chapter 2

WHAT'S YOUR POISON?

We all know that alcohol isn't good for us, so why do we drink? Let's take a look at the common misconceptions that drive people into the drinking trap and keep them there.

Why does anybody start drinking? There has been a lot of publicity about the disastrous effects caused by alcohol. Nobody can deny that, even in so-called "normal" drinkers, it debilitates bodily functions, in particular the senses and coordination. Recent studies concluded that there is no safe level of alcohol consumption.

Alcohol is a poison, and that's exactly how it tastes to us when we take those first experimental sips. Look at the faces of first-time drinkers. Remember how hard you had to work to get over the impulse to gag? But we persevere, determined to "acquire the taste." What we're actually doing is acquiring a loss of taste.

Like all animals, we are given a set of tools to help us distinguish food and drinks that are good for us from those that are poisonous. Our senses are designed to warn us off poisons, and that is exactly what they do when we have those first drinks.

The smell is repulsive. The taste is even worse. All our instincts are screaming: AVOID! But we don't pay attention to our instincts. We persevere, and then another survival tool kicks in. We vomit. The human body is designed to expel poison in whatever way it can. It's unpleasant, but our body is trying to do us a favor.

But even after vomiting, the temptation to drink remains strong. Why? What is it about this poison that keeps us coming back for more?

The truth is, there is nothing special about alcohol. It is all a myth. And one thing that sets humans apart from the rest of the animal kingdom is our susceptibility to myths.

Wild animals would probably not persist beyond smelling the stuff. Even if they got as far as tasting it, they wouldn't keep drinking it until they vomited. Of course we've all seen the wildlife programs showing animals "getting drunk" on naturally occurring alcohol in fermented fruit, but that behavior is an aberration. The limited studies that have been conducted on the issue indicate that animals either have no interest in alcohol or a distinct aversion to it. The exception being those animals whose diet is controlled by humans, who bizarrely give them alcohol. Drinking alcohol until you vomit is a uniquely human trait. Yet we think we're so much smarter than the rest of the animal kingdom.

WHY WE CONTINUE TO DRINK

We have senses, just as other animals do. They are an important part of our natural survival kit. But we have something that sets us apart from other animals: intellect.

Human beings have the mental power to reason, communicate, imagine, project, invent, and much more. It is this power that has given us control over other animals—and it is this power that causes us to believe myths that lead us into traps.

It's impossible to avoid the myths that surround alcohol. We are exposed to them from birth. We see our parents drink; we see celebrities drink; we see ads for alcoholic beverages; and we are raised to think that alcohol has a magical quality.

It's this brainwashing that compels us to drink in the first place; it's addiction that makes us keep drinking.

WHAT WE GET FROM DRINKING

So what are these wonderful benefits that we grow up believing alcohol will give us? Let's look at four of the most common myths.

1. IT'S A SOCIABLE DRUG

Somehow, alcohol has never gotten the bad press that other drugs do. In most countries it's legal, for one thing! Sure, we know it causes immense physical and social harm, but that just applies to people who can't handle it, right?

For the rest of us it's a social lubricant, the juice that makes the party swing. Want to be part of the "in crowd?" Grab a drink and join in!

Try throwing a party without alcohol and see what reception you get. We grow up assuming a party has to have alcohol for people to have a good time and we go on believing that myth, even when we know it doesn't give us a good time at all—quite the reverse in fact.

The fact is, alcohol is an incredibly antisocial drug. It debilitates our judgment, so we forget our manners and become rude, abusive loudmouths. It suppresses self-control, which leads to risky behavior or violence. And it knocks out our self-awareness, so we force all these things on others without realizing how antisocial we are being.

At its worst, drunkenness contributes to road deaths, sexual abuse, domestic violence, and a host of other forms of violence. Yet the myth machine cons us into believing that alcohol is a sociable drug.

2. IT HELPS YOU UNWIND

Whether it's a party, a vacation or just putting your feet up at the end of a long, hard day, when it comes to unwinding, alcohol is never far away.

We are sold the myth that alcohol helps you relax. In fact, it does the opposite. The nature of addiction is to always leave you wanting more. Until you get your next fix, you can't relax. Withdrawal from the drug puts you on edge, and the only thing that momentarily relieves that edginess is to drink more.

If you think alcohol helps you relax, it's because you drank it on occasions when you were relaxing anyway. A party? A vacation? The end of a long, hard day? Aren't these times when you relax anyway? You don't need alcohol to help you. In fact, it hinders you.

Try drinking in the midst of a truly stressful situation. For instance at work, when the pressure's on. Can you imagine how people would react? Would they say, "Oh, they're just having a drink so they can relax and handle the situation more calmly"?

Or would they say, "Wow! They must be losing it under all this pressure!"? If you drink alcohol to relax, it's because alcohol has made you permanently unrelaxed. I will explain this in more detail later.

3. IT GIVES US CONFIDENCE

This is the big draw for young, novice drinkers. Confidence is everything when you're a teenager, trying to understand your place in the world, trying to make friends with the people around you, trying to find love, identity, and respect.

Along comes booze which magically takes away all your inhibitions. But that's not the same as giving you confidence. Confidence is feeling secure enough in your natural state not to need a drug like alcohol to take away your inhibitions. Confidence is trusting in your personality to draw people to you.

Alcohol gives people misplaced confidence, which can be catastrophic. The teenager who decides to take a short-cut across the railroad tracks on their way home. The young person who accepts a ride from a stranger at the end of the night. Our inhibitions protect us from risking tragic outcomes. OK, it might feel like they are holding us back, but with practice we can learn to manage them and have a great time, without the fog of alcohol luring us into danger.

Alcohol actually destroys our confidence. Once strong, outgoing, and energetic people are reduced to physical and mental wrecks, fraught with anxiety.

4. IT'S A GROWN-UP THING TO DO

As we develop in adolescence and approach adulthood, we naturally adopt behaviors that we think make us look like adults. Smoking and drinking are two classic activities that young people adopt for no other reason than to appear grown up.

But let's examine that closer: what does being grown up really mean? Does it mean you're strong? Does it mean you're smart? This is how we want to be perceived as we approach adulthood, but we are misled once again by a myth.

Ask any emotional drinker, "Do you feel strong? Do you feel smart?" We all know the answer to these questions.

AMANDA'S STORY

"I started drinking when I was 16, which was pretty much the norm among my friends. I was a shy girl, self-conscious and quiet, and I saw other people who just seemed to ooze confidence. I started going to parties, and I would just stand there with my back against the wall, avoiding eye contact with any boys—and most of the girls, too.

"I remember being given my first drink—it was one of those 'hard seltzers.' It was sweet, but I found it pretty unpleasant. I drank it, though, and I found myself talking to all sorts of people. I thought, 'This is it! This is the confidence I've been searching for.'

"After that, I never went out anywhere without preloading with a few vodkas. People said they didn't recognize me when I was out and about—the party girl. I took it as a compliment, but now I'm not so sure. I think they sensed that I was out of control.

"By my mid-20s, I would say I was probably an alcoholic, although I wouldn't have admitted it at the time. I certainly relied on drink for all sorts of occasions: going out, staying in, seeing friends, being alone... that was my lifestyle.

"When I was 26, I got fired from my job for drinking at work. I used to keep a bottle of vodka in my desk drawer for social occasions, but I had started taking sips when I was feeling stressed. I didn't realize the effect it was having on me—but everyone else did. Apparently, it was really obvious. And it made me unemployable.

"I look back now on those 10 years, from my first drink to the day I got fired, and I realize I was living under an illusion. Nothing I did was real—not the real me, anyway. You could say I lost 10 years of my life. Thanks to Allen Carr, I'm just starting to put it back together now."

Amanda's story underlines the fact that there are no genuine benefits to drinking. Any benefit we think is there is a myth. These myths entice us into a trap from which escape seems impossible.

The good news is that escape is possible: it's even easy when you follow this method. But until you see the truth, addictive drugs such as alcohol create an illusion that keeps you trapped: the illusion of pleasure.

THE ILLUSION OF PLEASURE

What if Amanda had been able to see that the arguments for drinking were all false? What if the alcohol industry announced that these were just myths it had conjured up to sell more booze? Would that have cured her drinking problem?

The answer, unfortunately, is no. Because while it's these myths that lead us to drink in the first place, they are not the reason we get hooked. The real reason is that we genuinely believe that alcohol is giving us some sort of pleasure or comfort.

We can't define what that pleasure or comfort is; we just know it's there. And as long as it's there, we find it impossible to free ourselves from the desire to drink.

Starting in childhood, we are brainwashed into thinking that alcohol has magical properties, such as giving you confidence, helping you unwind, making you more sociable, etc. We are "treated" to alcohol on special occasions, which makes us feel grown up. The message is clear: this stuff is special.

Later in life, when we're feeling low, we seek comfort from alcohol. As an adult, you can indulge your need whenever you feel like it. And the more you indulge yourself, the more you feel like it.

BECAUSE IT'S ADDICTIVE!

It's like an itch that you can't resist scratching. If you don't scratch it, then the itch nags at you; if you do, the itch gets worse. As long as you believe that the only way to stop the itch is to scratch it, you will keep scratching and the itch will keep getting worse.

As the itch gets worse, your scratching becomes less effective. So you have to scratch harder. The scratching isn't making you happy and relaxed, but you're convinced that if you don't scratch, the itch will be unbearable.

Addiction traps you in a cycle of trying to get relief by using the very thing that's causing you misery. It plays tricks on your mind and creates its own need. The only way to stop the cycle of misery is to stop scratching the itch.

The "pleasure" you think you get from alcohol is an illusion created by addiction. So how can you tell real pleasure from illusory pleasure? Later in the book I will give you a practical demonstration that will show you how. For now, all you need to do is change your perception of alcohol and what it does for you. To do that, you need to follow the second instruction.

SECOND INSTRUCTION: OPEN YOUR MIND.

You may already regard yourself as an open-minded person. However, the fact is we go through life with our minds largely made up by other people. When you see the sun rise in the morning, you regard it as a ball of fiery gases burning millions of miles away, which has the appearance of rising in the sky because the Earth is turning. But how do you know that's the case? Isn't it because you've been presented with some very convincing arguments by people you regard as experts in that field, and the explanation tallies with what you see with your own eyes?

But not very long ago, people were convinced that the sun was actually a god driving a fiery chariot across the sky. That was the explanation put forward by the learned men of the time, and it tallied with what people saw.

Now take a look at the picture of what appear to be a short man, a medium one, and a tall one below.

If I were to tell you that the men in this drawing were, in fact, all exactly the same size, you'd dispute that, wouldn't you? The fact is, they *are* all identical. Take a ruler and measure them if you need to be convinced.

This illusion demonstrates how our minds can easily be tricked into accepting false "facts." Firstly, I implied that they were different sizes and what you saw appeared to confirm that. When you first started drinking, you probably believed you were exercising your freedom to choose when and what you drank, but what if you were basing your choice on false information? What if all those benefits you believed you were buying into were actually illusions created by brainwashing?

As you continue through the book, remember this diagram of the three men and keep an open mind, so that even if I tell you something you find difficult to believe, you will at least accept the possibility that it is true.

Chapter 3

WHY YOU'RE READING THIS BOOK

IN THIS CHAPTER
•*THE BRAINWASHING* •*LEARNING FROM FAILURE*
•*HOW MUCH WILLPOWER DO YOU NEED?*
•*WHO AM I WITHOUT BOOZE?* •*DENIAL* •*THE EASY OPTION*

Do you find that whenever you're not drinking, you always have alcohol on your mind, but whenever you are drinking, you wish you weren't? This is the paradox of emotional drinking. Why is it so hard to stop even when you derive no pleasure from it?

There is no pleasure in drinking. You drink merely to satisfy a craving and, every time you do, it makes you miserable and you desperately wish you could quit. The excitement we feel as young adults going out is long since gone, and drinking is now just a mundane experience, leaving you with a low, sinking feeling.

So if it's such a miserable experience, why don't drinkers just stop doing it?

THE BRAINWASHING

The reason for this mystifying state of affairs lies in the way our brains are wired. There is the rational mind, which may tell you that alcohol is a poison and drinking is causing you embarrassment, harm, and misery, so you should stop. But then there is the emotive mind, which continues to crave alcohol.

Why? Because it has been conditioned to believe that alcohol is the only thing that can give you pleasure or comfort.

This creates a tug-of-war between two fears: the fear of what emotional drinking is doing to you versus the fear of life without that which you have come to regard as your crutch.

It's a revelation to a lot of people when it's pointed out to them that both sides of this tug-of-war are caused by the same thing: emotional drinking. Once you understand how you've been fooled into believing that alcohol provides a pleasure or crutch, both fears are removed. Suddenly it becomes obvious that there is one simple way to break free, and that is to follow your rational mind and stop drinking.

This is the easy way. It just requires you to undo the brainwashing that has created the desire for alcohol.

Before you can begin this process, however, you need to make sure you're in the right frame of mind. That means two things:

1. Recognize and accept that you have been brainwashed.

2. Take a positive attitude to escaping from the trap.

One difference between Easyway and other methods that claim to help overcome addiction is that the other methods begin with the message that it will <u>not</u> be easy. This just adds to the brainwashing that keeps addicts in the trap, because the harder you think quitting is going to be, the more fearful you will be of trying and the more you will seek comfort in "the devil you know."

THE BELIEF THAT QUITTING WILL BE HARD KEEPS EMOTIONAL DRINKERS IN THE TRAP, DESPITE KNOWING THAT IT IS DOING THEM HARM.

The obvious question is this:

IF IT'S EASY TO STOP, WHY DOESN'T EVERYONE DO IT?

It's important to ask questions like this, and not just swallow everything you're told. I want you to question everything you're told about drinking alcohol, and that includes everything you've been told in the past. When you question things, the truth is revealed. The problem is that most of us never question the information we're given about alcohol, from generation to generation.

Easyway works. Tens of millions of ex-addicts around the world can vouch for that. At this stage it doesn't matter if you're ready to believe it will work for you or not; all that matters is that you follow the instructions. After all, what do you have to lose? Further loss of control, the deterioration of your health, and more misery? Let's examine the reasons why you believe quitting will be hard.

WHAT WE LEARN FROM FAILURE

You probably know of other people who have tried to get their drinking under control but failed. Maybe you've tried, but found yourself pulled back into the trap by a force that was too strong for you to overcome.

Every failed attempt to quit drinking is damaging for two reasons. The first is the effect it has on your self-esteem. Already low because of the helplessness you feel as an addict, your self-esteem takes a further hit with every failure. You interpret it as evidence that you are not made of the right stuff for taking control of this problem.

Secondly, failure reinforces your belief that your addiction is like an impregnable prison from which it is incredibly hard, perhaps even impossible, to escape.

This second impression can be caused not just by your own failure to quit, but also by the failure of others. Every time you hear of someone who has made an attempt to quit drinking but failed, or you see someone drinking whom you thought had quit, it strengthens the illusion that perhaps you can never be free.

When you look at these people, and even when you look at yourself, you see someone who is, in many ways, strong. There is no "type" that becomes an addict because they are weak or foolish or too stupid to see their way out of their problem. Many highly intelligent, single-minded, brave, and strong people have endured the misery of addiction and found it impossible to escape. But the reason they find it so difficult to escape is not because it is actually difficult; it's simply because they are going about it the wrong way.

HOW MUCH WILLPOWER DO YOU NEED?

In order to escape the trap, you have to have a positive attitude. You might interpret that as "I need to muster all my willpower." This is a common misconception, and one that actually drives addicts further into the trap. I will go into this in greater detail later, but for now just consider the idea that you do not need willpower to overcome your alcohol issue.

People who try to quit drinking and fail usually assume that they have failed because they lack the willpower to resist the temptation to drink. They believe that it must be some weakness on their part that prevents them from quitting permanently.

This is another misconception that is put in your mind by brainwashing—and not only by the people who want you to remain addicted. Most methods that claim to help with addictions begin from the position that willpower is essential. Easyway has always been the one method that does not. It also happens to be the most effective method ever devised.

I said that this book will help you overcome your emotional drinking without any sense of sacrifice or deprivation. When you reach the end and experience the elation of finding yourself free, you'll know exactly what I mean. Right now, however, you might still be finding it hard to believe that it is possible to overcome your issues with alcohol without huge amounts of willpower, a feeling of immense sacrifice, and a painful period of withdrawal.

So you have a simple choice:

1. Keep reading, follow the instructions, and see if my claims are valid;

OR

2. Continue the way you're going now, suffering the misery of emotional drinking, falling deeper and deeper into the trap, losing your health, your vitality, your body shape, your self-respect, and becoming increasingly resigned to a miserable life... and death.

If you think you've failed to quit in the past because you lack willpower, I have nothing but good news. Willpower didn't come into it. You failed to quit because you were using a method that does not work. By picking up this book, you have embarked on a method that has already been proven to work by millions of people all over the world.

Whether it's alcohol addiction, nicotine, cocaine, heroin, cannabis, prescription drugs, or sugar (all of which are perceived as mainly physical addictions), or gambling, junk spending, digital/tech addiction, or emotional eating (all mostly perceived as mainly mental addictions), this method has set an estimated 50 million people free. Easily! All you have to do is keep reading and following all the instructions. It really is as simple as that!

WHO AM I WITHOUT BOOZE?

That might sound like a weird question, but for many problem drinkers, their reputation for boozing can feel like a key part of their identity. While some emotional drinkers try to keep their drinking secret, others show off their excess to get a laugh. It becomes a badge of honor: "She's the one who's always got a glass of wine in her hand—the life and soul of the party."

This just shows how addiction can twist your mind. You overlook the misery, the poor health, the torment, the self-loathing, and instead see your problem as some sort of charisma. You make the mistake of thinking people respect you for it or find you interesting and quirky because of it.

Of course, you know that's not the real state of affairs. Emotional drinkers are anything but happy-go-lucky. They constantly worry about their alcohol consumption, about the physical and mental effects, the anxiety they feel "the morning after," the health implications, and the slavery.

But we are brainwashed with the stereotypes so consistently, it's not surprising that our own self-image often appears more attractive if there are obvious flaws. We worry that if we take alcohol out of our life, we will lose what we perceive to be our "charm" or sense of self.

Yet you spend most of your time trying to conceal the fact that you have an issue with alcohol. You put on a brave, smiling face to cover up the misery and confusion. But underneath, you are ashamed of the way alcohol has a hold on you. You don't want everybody to know that you've lost control, that you've lost the ability to enjoy life, and that you're stuck in a trap from which you feel incapable of escape.

You know the truth: there is nothing charming or fun about being addicted to alcohol. The effects on your physical health are depressing at best, devastating at worst. The effect on your mental health is to plunge you into a spiral of misery and confusion.

IN HIS OWN WORDS: SIMON

"I wasn't a big drinker in my teens. I was athletic, and I knew that alcohol was the enemy of performance. If my friends back then knew that I had developed a problem with booze, they would be amazed. I rarely touched the stuff.

"The fact is, I've learned that there is no typical 'type' when it comes to emotional drinking. Anyone can get caught in that trap. For me, the thing that changed in my life was an injury. I was a promising football player, and my dream was to turn pro. But at 19 I suffered a knee injury that put an end to that.

"For me, it felt like the end of the world. Football had been my life and, I thought, my future. Now what did I have? I needed something to fill the vacuum. And I thought about all the drinking I had avoided in order to stay fit and healthy and I thought, 'I don't need to miss out any more.' So I started drinking... and drinking... and drinking.

"From football player to drinker. That was my identity shift. The obvious difference being that football had been a genuine pleasure that kept me healthy and happy, whereas drinking was an illusory pleasure that always left me feeling down. But whenever I felt down, the only thing I wanted was another drink.

"People find it hard to understand how a physically fit young man with a passion can suddenly let himself go, gain weight, and lose interest in life. They think you would stop when you see the signs—the beer belly, the woozy head, the sluggishness. But by the time you see the signs, you're well and truly in the trap. The signs just add to your misery, which adds to the compulsion to drink.

"Thanks to Easyway, though, I did stop. I was taken there by a good friend, who had been through the same thing and recognized the problem in me. Until then, I thought I was the problem. I knew I had felt sorry for myself over the injury, and I assumed that self-pity, not alcohol, was my problem. After all, everyone else seemed to be able to drink without it causing problems.

"So I continued to seek comfort in drinking, not realizing that it was the cause of my misery. And the one or two occasions when I did try to stop, and failed, I naturally blamed myself.

"But going to Easyway changed my mindset. I realized the problem was not me, it was alcohol, pure and simple. My addiction to alcohol was making me miserable. The way they explained it made perfect sense. It was a huge boost, because it gave me the absolute belief that I could quit drinking and my life would be much better for it.

"And so it has proved. I'm fit and healthy again and, while I'm not playing football any more, there are plenty of other sports I can enjoy. And boy do I enjoy them! To think that I ever regarded alcohol as my one and only source of pleasure. It's ridiculous. But when you're in the trap, you just don't see things as they really are."

DENIAL

Everyone with an alcohol issue wishes they could stop. The fact that they find themselves incapable of doing so makes them feel foolish and weak, so they try to make themselves feel better by coming up with excuses for why they continue to drink.

"It's just the way I'm made."

"Life would be pretty dull without it."

"I can stop any time I like."

"I need to let my hair down."

These are classic examples of how addicts delude themselves. They all imply that you have made a controlled choice to drink. But as everyone with a drinking issue knows:

YOU DON'T CONTROL EMOTIONAL DRINKING; IT CONTROLS YOU.

All addictions are predominantly mental. Emotional drinking is a cycle of control and abandonment of control. If you deny yourself a drink for a period of time, the exercise of control can be the addictive element because you can feel your willpower apparently giving you control. But when willpower gives out, as it inevitably does, the surrender of control can give you a sense of release.

For many problem drinkers, it is the combination of both extremes that keeps them hooked, in addition to the addictive properties of the drug itself.

The three elements of emotional drinking can be defined as:

1. Exercise of control NOT to drink;

2. Abandonment of control, surrendering to the urge to drink;

3. Addiction to alcohol.

The first element—using willpower and self-discipline to resist bingeing on alcohol—can be exhausting, impossible to maintain, and therefore destined to fail. When you understand how you have become addicted, you'll realize that willpower and self-discipline have no part in your cure, because the temptation to drink will be removed altogether.

The second element, the surrender, is riddled with mixed emotions. The relief of abandoning self-control can be intoxicating, but it is counterbalanced by the self-loathing of giving in. A high coupled with a deep, anxious low. No wonder emotional drinking leaves you feeling absolutely bewildered and helpless!

The ultimate result of bingeing on booze, though, is a physical and emotional low. Eventually you try to exert control again. And so the cycle continues, lurching from apparent control to surrender. Sometimes you feel like you're winning, sometimes you know you're losing.

The fact is, you're never winning, because those moments of control are all part of the addiction cycle—the third element. Without overcoming the addiction you will be forever doomed to the exhausting cycle of emotional drinking.

If you recognize this pattern, I have good news for you: freedom awaits.

When you find yourself in a trap, it's frightening to admit it because it forces you to face two options: stay in the trap and continue to suffer, or escape. Attempting to escape can seem more frightening than staying in the trap if you've been brainwashed into believing it will be a difficult, painful, and perhaps impossible process. Faced with that prospect, the familiarity of the trap seems like the lesser of two evils.

But when you realize that escaping doesn't need to be painful or difficult, the situation changes completely. Rather than facing two evils in a tug-of-war, you find yourself facing one evil and one easy, happy option. That's when escape becomes easy.

THE EASY OPTION

You have a pretty good idea of what life will be like if you choose to remain in the trap: more physical degradation and more mental torment. Now let's take a look at the life that awaits you when you're free of emotional drinking.

HEALTH

Emotional drinking deteriorates your health, both mentally and physically. It's common to put on weight, which puts a strain on your vital organs, including your heart and lungs, making the simplest physical tasks feel like hard work. It also creates an addiction cycle in your mind, making it impossible to enjoy genuine pleasures because your brain is always craving the "reward" of your alcohol fix. The combination of physical and mental suffering can cause sleep deprivation. And the worse you feel, the more you tend to neglect every aspect of your health. Maybe you retain the consolation that , as a result of endless gym visits, you remain in pretty good shape? But, deep down, you sense that the workouts are getting harder and harder, and the physical and aesthetic consequences of drinking are becoming increasingly difficult to conceal.

When you're free from the tyranny of emotional drinking, you will start to feel fitter and more energetic, you will sleep more soundly, and generally feel a fantastic glow of health and happiness. In addition to the improvement in your physical health, your mental health will improve. You'll feel released from the dark cloud of repetitive bingeing and bouts of apparent control, and from the constant feelings of failure, shame, and low self-esteem. It feels like escaping from a cold, dark prison cell into sunshine, blue sky, and freedom.

CONTROL

When you regain control over alcohol you will feel much better about every aspect of yourself. You will recognize that you are strong, and that you have the ability to make decisions that govern your life and happiness. You will be able relax, free from the constant struggle with alcohol.

The best thing about being in control is that you do not have to think about it, as you do when wrestling to control your drinking. You will enjoy "not being out of control" without feeling like you're having to try constantly to remain in control. You'll just be leading a natural, healthy life.

Think about non-drinkers now. Do they need to exercise control not to drink? Not at all. The thought doesn't enter their mind. They control alcohol by not inviting it into their life in the first place.

HONESTY

It's hard work covering up an addiction. All that denial requires a lot of untruths. Free from emotional drinking, you will no longer feel ashamed and compelled to cover up. As a result, you will feel far less stressed and defensive, and you'll be able to lead your life freely with your head held high.

SELF-RESPECT

Your new, calmer and more contented lifestyle and the realization that you are no longer a slave to booze will make you feel much better about yourself. Every time you think about your achievement in escaping the trap, you will feel a burst of elation and pride, and you'll love weekend mornings free from alcohol-induced anxiety and illness.

TIME

When you no longer spend your life obsessing about drinking, whether you're trying to get a drink or trying to hide your drinking, you will find you have much more time to pursue things that are truly worthwhile—things you genuinely enjoy, like exercising or just relaxing with family or friends.

MONEY

Emotional drinking is expensive. You can look forward to having much more disposable income when you're not blowing your money on booze—not to mention cabs.

You have all these benefits, and many more, to look forward to when you walk out of the trap that is emotional drinking. In order to get there, you don't need willpower, nor to fight your way through a painful period of withdrawal. All you need to do is keep a positive mindset and methodically unravel the illusions that have put you in the trap in the first place.

It's a simple case of following instructions. So if you're worried that you're about to be forced to go through some awful trauma, or sacrifice something that is truly precious to you, put that thought out of your mind and replace it with the thought of all the wonderful benefits you will soon be enjoying.

THIRD INSTRUCTION: BEGIN WITH A FEELING OF ELATION.

Chapter 4

FIRST STEPS
TO FREEDOM

IN THIS CHAPTER
•NO MAGIC, NO MIRACLES •HOW EASYWAY WORKS
•QUITTING IS NOT ENOUGH •FALSE IMPRESSION

The mindset that keeps you trapped in the misery of emotional drinking is built on illusions. There is nothing to fear from life without alcohol. Escaping the trap is easy and you have nothing to feel miserable about. This is the truth: now all we need to do is help you understand it and acknowledge it.

When you're desperate to cure an issue like emotional drinking, you can start to believe that the only thing that will help you is a miracle. There have been a lot of things written about Easyway over the years, mostly from former addicts writing enthusiastically about how incredibly effective the method is.

You may have read that Easyway works like magic, and I'm sure you're eager to discover the secret of this magical cure. In fact, you're probably wondering why I don't just tell you the magic formula right now. Please don't be misled:

1. It is not a secret.

2. There is no magic, even if there seems to be.

Easyway actually works in an incredibly straightforward way, by using indisputable logic to strip away illusions put into your mind by brainwashing and replace those illusions with rational thought, which removes your desire to take alcohol for emotional relief. The key is the set of instructions you receive throughout the book, and it must be used like the combination lock of a safe. Each step must be understood and applied in order for the combination to work.

You have already been given the first three instructions and your escape plan is under way, but please be patient. The key to your escape does not lie in the final chapter or the first chapter, or any other single chapter; the whole book is the key.

HOW EASYWAY WORKS

This method works by removing your desire to drink alcohol in response to certain emotions. In order to do that, we need to change your understanding of the relationship between alcohol and emotions. What is it that makes you an emotional drinker? Something in your DNA?

No. It's a subtle combination of addiction to alcohol, the exercise of control NOT to binge, and the surrendering of control that leads to a binge. You might be surprised to learn that exercising control to stop bingeing is part of the problem. After all, isn't emotional drinking brought on by a lack of control? Without periods of apparent control, there cannot be loss of control. The two go hand in hand.

Emotional drinking is characterized by a pattern of highs and lows. There are periods of *restraint*, during which you might feel deprived and miserable, interrupted by spells of *loss of restraint*, which leave you feeling worse.

The loss of restraint drags you down ever lower, leaving you feeling helpless and worthless. When the binge ends and you re-establish restraint, it feels like a lift and a sort of comfort. You might call it a peak, but all it really is is a return to something close to normality.

Limiting your intake by willpower is exhausting because you're having to exercise enormous self-control, putting you in a constant state of deprivation, feeling like you're making a sacrifice and missing out, while at the same time regretting those spells of lost restraint, which leave you full of self-loathing.

There really aren't many happy moments for emotional drinkers.

Mixed into this cocktail of mental torture is the effect of alcohol addiction, which causes spikes and crashes in your emotional condition. These seemingly converse sensations are characteristic of addiction in general. Cocaine addicts often take cocaine (a stimulant) with alcohol (a depressant) in a deliberate attempt to counteract one with the other. They'll say, "I take coke to help me sober up so I can drink more, and then I drink booze to take the edge off the coke."

Emotional drinkers are in an almost constant state of misery and discomfort, even though the alcohol binges may be sporadic. Either they feel deprived because they are denying themselves their little crutch, or they feel weak because they have lost control again. Add to this the debilitating physical and mental effects of alcohol and the picture really is quite grim.

Luckily, with Easyway, soon you'll be able to escape from the whole nightmare. The key to your escape is to understand that controlling your drinking through sheer willpower is not helpful. Instead you want to *allow yourself not to drink alcohol,* because it is infinitely preferable to drinking it.

Can you see how a simple shift in attitude takes away the need for willpower?

FALLING BACK IN

An addict is caught in a trap. Between us we have the two essentials that will set you free: you have a strong desire to get out, and I have the key that will make that possible. All you have to do is follow my instructions.

However, once you are released, there is a further danger: the trap still exists, and we have to ensure that you don't fall into it again.

QUITTING IS NOT ENOUGH

Addicts are notorious for stopping and starting again. They're always wanting to quit, so they make a big effort to stop or cut down and then, when they feel they've regained some control, they reward themselves with a drink. "Just one; what's the harm?" The harm is that "just one" is all it takes to push you back into the trap.

So helping you escape the trap is not enough; we need to ensure that you never fall into it again by permanently removing your desire to drink.

We can do this by enabling you to understand the nature of the trap. It is not something that is commonly talked about. We don't like to think that we might be caught in a trap; we like to think we're in control, so we keep it to ourselves and allow the brainwashing to go unchallenged, warping our perception. But until you recognize the trap and remove the brainwashing, you cannot truly escape the slavery of being an emotional drinker.

Unlike a cage, the trap you're in is not physical but psychological. In other words, it exists entirely in your mind. It is an illusion conjured up by brainwashing.

THE TRAP IS EASY TO FALL INTO...
FORTUNATELY IT'S ALSO EASY TO ESCAPE.

Remember the illusion of the three men in chapter two? It's very easy to be convinced that what you're seeing is not actually what is there. All it takes is one false piece of information. Do you remember how I implied that the three men were different size? When it comes to alcohol, you have been brainwashed with numerous false impressions for years, and these have created the illusion that you get some sort of pleasure or comfort from it. Therefore, you believe that quitting involves making a sacrifice.

It's a confidence trick. Once you can see through a confidence trick, you will never fall for it again. Try turning back to that illustration with the knowledge you have now. Can you convince yourself that the men are not identical?

You may wonder why brainwashing traps some people and not others. Billions of people have lived their lives without ever falling into the emotional drinking trap, even though they, too, have been subjected to brainwashing from a young age.

One theory is that some people are born with an addictive personality. In other words, something in their mentality makes them more vulnerable to falling into the trap. The addictive personality theory is frequently cited, as if it were a proven fact, but it is nothing more than a theory and, as I will show you later, there is much ammunition with which to shoot it down. Furthermore, it is of no help whatsoever to addicts trying to escape the trap.

The fact is, anybody can fall into the trap and anybody can escape. It's a simple question of understanding what it is that makes you fall in and what it is that keeps you there.

No one forces you to drink. It's you who makes that choice. The fact that part of your brain wishes you didn't, or can't understand why you do, doesn't change the situation. You drink because you have a desire to do so. That desire is what makes you feel deprived when you force yourself to do without. It is what makes you feel agitated when you see other people drinking and you can't. Desire is what drags you back into the trap just when you think you've escaped.

IN ORDER TO STAY OUT OF THE TRAP PERMANENTLY, YOU NEED TO REMOVE THE DESIRE TO DRINK.

The only difference between emotional drinkers and non-drinkers who aren't suffering that misery is that the latter don't have the same desire for alcohol as an emotional crutch. That is not to say they are immune to brainwashing. Many of them probably believe that there is some pleasure or comfort to be gained from alcohol. There may come a time in their lives when they are feeling low and need something to pick them up, and they may fall into the trap then, too.

Anyone with a clear mind who weighs up objectively the pros and cons of drinking will reach the conclusion that it is a fool's game. People who have no desire for alcohol are able to make that rational decision. They are able to maintain the power of reason over temptation because their reasoning has not been affected by addiction.

You may interpret that to mean your situation is desperate because you are in no position to apply that sort of clear-headed reasoning, but I have good news for you: you don't need to.

EASYWAY DOES NOT REQUIRE THE POWER OF REASON TO OUTWEIGH TEMPTATION; IT REMOVES TEMPTATION ALTOGETHER.

People who have never fallen into the trap are still susceptible to the illusion that there is some pleasure or comfort to be derived from drinking alcohol. There is no guarantee that at some point in the future they won't succumb to brainwashing and fall into the trap themselves.

But when you've been in the trap and then removed the brainwashing, you are in a stronger position than someone who has never been trapped: you are no longer susceptible to the illusions. You KNOW that there is no pleasure or comfort in emotional drinking. Therefore, your desire is removed for good.

The only relevant difference between you and someone who does not try to use alcohol for emotional support is that they don't have the desire to do so. Neither did you until you fell into the trap.

THE ADDICTION CREATES THE DESIRE.

Remember, addicts seek comfort in the very thing that's causing them misery. They just can't see the connection. This is the trap you are in. It is a vicious circle, which you can break by opening your mind and unraveling the brainwashing.

Thanks to Easyway, there are large numbers of former addicts who once thought they could never break free from the trap they were in, but have now escaped and have no desire to fall back in. Soon you will join them. Please don't worry if that thought seems scary—that's perfectly normal. All you need to do is keep reading and follow the instructions.

FALSE IMPRESSION

Here's a description of one of the world's most common addictive substances:

- It's well-known for its harmful effects on the human body.

- It usually hooks its victims immediately and in many cases they remain hooked for life.

- Dealers hook users and keep them hooked with cheap deals.

- The more miserable it makes you, the greater your dependency on it becomes.

- Side effects include sluggishness, depression, stress, anxiety, loss of self-esteem, shame, guilt, destitution, dishonesty, financial ruin, isolation, and sometimes suicide.

- Benefits: none.

This may sound like a description of heroin. In fact, it's a description of alcohol. But it's not the popular image of booze, is it? The way alcohol is marketed to us is completely different. Happy, beautiful people having fun or acting cool and sophisticated, showing no signs of weight gain, strain or anxiety, enjoying all the pleasures that life has to offer. The message is straightforward: "Alcohol makes you happy."

Do you agree with that? I assume you don't, which is why you're reading this book. It's time to dispel these illusions once and for all, so that instead of seeing drinking as a pleasure or comfort, you will see the true picture, just as you do with heroin. By the time you finish the book, your frame of mind will be such that, whenever you think about drinking, instead of feeling deprived because you can no longer drink, you will feel overjoyed because you no longer have to.

You need to understand that the trap you're in as an emotional drinker is the same as that of a heroin addict. It is a mental trap, not a physical one, and it is created by brainwashing. In order to escape, you need to change your frame of mind. First it is essential to realize that you are in the trap.

If you can look at a heroin addict and see the mistake he is making in thinking the next fix will make everything all right, you are already on the way to solving your own problem. The goal of this book is to help you reverse the brainwashing that has led you into the emotional drinking trap. It will help you see that drinking does not relieve your misery; it is the cause of it. There is no need for you to be miserable. The life of someone free from the burden of emotional drinking awaits you very soon. You have every reason to feel excited.

As you read through this book, we will remove these illusions from your brain so that, instead of seeing emotional drinking as a pleasure or comfort, you start to see the true picture, just as you can with heroin. By the time you finish the book, you will have the right frame of mind so that whenever you think about taking alcohol for emotional support, instead of feeling deprived because *you can no longer do so,* you will feel overjoyed because *you no longer have to.*

Chapter 5

THE TRAP

I have described emotional drinking as a trap, in which the more you struggle to break free, the more tightly ensnared you become. In order to escape, you need to understand how this trap works.

We all know that alcohol is an addictive drug, but many emotional drinkers still find it hard to accept that they are addicted. When they think of addicts, they think of heroin users or chain smokers.

Only 50 years ago, the majority of the adult population felt the same way about smoking. Even in the early days of Easyway, back in the late 1980s, we faced quite a challenge convincing smokers that they were, in fact, addicted to nicotine. They looked at their addiction in the same way as they might regard a "golf addict" or a "TV addict"—more a case of liking it a lot, rather than being clinically hooked. They were extremely resistant to the notion that they smoked because they were addicted to nicotine.

These days, smokers are more accepting of that fact; the only challenge that remains for us is to help them understand that it's their addiction that convinces them that they derive some sort of pleasure or crutch from smoking.

Addiction is a con trick that fools otherwise intelligent, logical people into thinking that they get something positive from a substance that:

a)   Creates undesirable withdrawal symptoms when it is first taken;

b)   Partially relieves those undesirable   symptoms when taken a second time...

c)   And a third time...

d)   And a fourth time, and so on.

The same pattern applies to nicotine, alcohol, and all addictive drugs, as well as addictive behaviors. It's the pattern of a lifetime of slavery. There is no genuine pleasure in addiction, any more than there is genuine pleasure in taking off tight shoes at the end of the day. It is merely relief from the discomfort that is brought on by taking the drug in the first place.

In the 1960s and 1970s, most adults smoked and, even though there was growing evidence that it caused cancer, they saw smoking as much safer than taking heroin. We now know that smoking is a far bigger killer than heroin. You might argue that's because far more people smoke than use heroin. OK, but why do people do either one when they know it could kill them? Is it because of the incredible pleasure or comfort they get from it? Or is it simply because they're addicted to the drug?

IT MAKES NO DIFFERENCE WHETHER YOU CHOOSE TO SEE YOUR PROBLEM AS ADDICTION. THE FACT OF THE MATTER IS THAT ALCOHOL TRAPS YOU IN A CYCLE OF CRAVING, DISSATISFACTION, ANXIETY, AND SELF-LOATHING IN EXACTLY THE SAME WAY AS HEROIN AND OTHER ADDICTIVE DRUGS.

Back when smoking was all the rage, we didn't know how nicotine and other drugs affected the brain. Since then, we have learned a great deal about a function of the brain known as "reward pathways." These are networks of transmitters and receptors in the brain that are connected by a hormone called dopamine. When dopamine makes a connection in the reward pathways, we feel good.

These pathways have an important role to play in encouraging us to do things that are good for us as a species. Exercise, laughter, sex, a hug, great music, and eating all cause dopamine to be released, and the feelings we experience incentivize us to keep doing things that are good for us. It's a simple survival mechanism.

However, drugs like heroin, nicotine, and alcohol disrupt this extraordinary, natural mechanism to the point where it ceases to register genuine pleasures at all unless they are combined with the drug.

THE TRUTH ABOUT DOPAMINE

As more and more becomes known about the way addictive drugs affect dopamine, science confirms what we've been saying at Easyway for more than 40 years. In 2019, Professor Robert West, one of the world's leading academics in the field of nicotine addiction, said this:

"Nicotine causes dopamine release by nerve cells in the *nucleus accumbens*, a part of the brain involved in learning to do things. The dopamine release tells the brain to pay attention to the situation and what the smoker was just doing—and to do the same thing the next time they're in that situation. So, a link is forged between the impulse to smoke and situations in which smoking normally happens."

Professor West went on to add, "Crucially, the smoker doesn't have to feel any pleasure or enjoyment for this to work."

Our first experience of alcohol is normally very unpleasant. Most of us remember that, which alone disproves the notion that alcohol causes "pleasure." Whatever impact it has on dopamine and the reward pathways when first introduced into your body, it's certainly not pleasurable.

In fact, most people's first taste of alcohol is so unpleasant and unrewarding that it convinces them they could never become addicted to it. The reason we develop a deep-seated belief that drinking *is* pleasurable is explained perfectly by Professor West.

POINT A

Alcohol withdrawal, a mild, empty, slightly insecure feeling, is the result of the first-ever alcoholic drink you had. It is temporarily "relieved" by the next drink. The brain concludes unconsciously, "Next time you feel alcohol withdrawal, do that again!" In other words, the behavior of having a drink in response to experiencing alcohol withdrawal is reinforced every time a drinker drinks, regardless of the fact that the next drink will also cause alcohol withdrawal.

Whether you're in a happy situation, a pressured situation, a relaxing situation, a social situation, or a lonely situation, you're also experiencing alcohol withdrawal. So responding by having a drink and immediately feeling a little better creates the illusion that alcohol has improved the situation. What you don't realize is that each drink will simply perpetuate the feeling of alcohol withdrawal.

This is why drinkers become convinced that alcohol helps them cope with sadness, boredom, loneliness, and stress, and makes good times feel better. It has nothing to do with genuine pleasure or genuine improvement of your mood. And every time you have a drink in those situations, your brain takes notice: "Next time that happens, do that again!"

Non-drinkers don't have to deal with any of the mental and physical aggravation caused by alcohol. They don't suffer from alcohol poisoning, withdrawal, or the suppression of genuine pleasures.

POINT B

All a drinker "enjoys" is relief from the empty, insecure feeling of alcohol withdrawal to regain the feeling of peace, calm, and relaxation they enjoyed all their life before taking that first experimental drink. In other words, a drinker drinks in order to feel like a non-drinker.

At our live seminars, once an alcohol addict understands Points A and B, we explain how the physical withdrawal from alcohol, irrespective of the drug's influence on dopamine levels, is actually extremely mild, and that the really unpleasant symptoms they, or any other drinker, experience when trying to quit with willpower are the result of a mental struggle. That struggle is caused by the drinker feeling deprived of what they think is their little crutch—a genuine pleasure or comfort.

We go on to reveal how the belief system surrounding alcohol—that it helps you relax, socialize, feel confident, cope with stress, have fun, etc.—is based on misinformation and misinterpretation of personal experiences, coupled with their addiction to alcohol.

The drinker can then see that there aren't any benefits to drinking and, therefore, there is no point doing it. This leaves them to handle the extremely mild symptoms of alcohol withdrawal without having to experience the torture of feeling that they are being deprived.

This is hugely important, because the now ex-drinker develops new responses to those old triggers, as described by Professor West. For example, if they used to pour a drink as soon as they got home from work, that moment might continue to trigger the thought of drinking in the first few weeks of being a happy non-drinker. But because they've quit with Easyway, instead of having to consciously process thoughts and feelings of loss and sacrifice, they process thoughts and feelings of release and freedom. You could say they "rewire" their brain. And it's not only easy, it's enjoyable.

Now apply this thinking to your own experiences. Think about your relationship with alcohol. When you've felt lonely or stressed or in need of a pick-me-up, which bottle have you reached for? Every time you've had a drink in response to feeling down, your brain has taken notice and concluded, subconsciously, "Next time you feel that way, DO THAT AGAIN!"

GENUINE PLEASURES

Drinking binges are always followed by feelings of misery, shame, remorse, guilt, and self-loathing. Emotional drinkers try to remedy these feelings by making a concerted mental effort to stay off the booze. It's the cycle I referred to earlier in terms of "exercising control not to binge."

Remember the three elements of emotional drinking addiction:

1. Exercise of control NOT to binge;

2. Abandonment of control, succumbing to the desire to binge;

3. Addiction to alcohol.

There are lots of wonderful, safe, healthy, and non-addictive ways to stimulate dopamine release for entirely positive effects. Many of them cost nothing: listening to music, dancing, cuddling, holding hands, laughing, or making love. Fortunately, the list is endless.

Each of these activities triggers dopamine release and leaves you feeling genuinely happier in a way that lasts. And they do not involve drug addiction or withdrawal symptoms or guilt. Rather than being a slave to something that makes you feel miserable, guilty, ashamed, sick, and full of self-loathing, you can fill your life with things that provide genuine pleasure.

These things are no secret. We know what genuine pleasures really are but addiction compels us to pursue illusory pleasure through drugs like alcohol and nicotine.

Once you unravel the brainwashing and reconnect with genuine pleasures, genuine sensations, and mindful sources of contentment, the idea of disrupting that by bingeing on booze and suffering all the horrible consequences of addiction becomes unthinkable.

After a tough day at work, what do you really think would make you feel better: alcohol or a lovely, long, comforting cuddle on the sofa with your partner? If you don't have a partner, a leisurely walk, a phone call with a friend, a luxurious bath, a hug with a friend... anything but booze will relax you far better.

If you have relationships to mend as a result of your emotional drinking, this book won't directly help you repair the wounds; but, like every addict Easyway has cured, you will find, once you've escaped from the trap, that you immediately feel better equipped to sort out other elements in your life that require attention.

Having said that, there is one relationship this book will definitely help you fix—the most important one there is: your relationship with yourself.

TIGHT SHOES

Any pick-me-up, any "high," any feeling of comfort you may have experienced when you've turned to alcohol to cope with unpleasant emotions has been fake. This "pleasure" you feel is the result of a fiendish combination of factors: repeated, prolonged periods of suffering (the exercising of apparent control over your drinking), followed by moments or periods of "release" (abandoning apparent control over your drinking) and the partial, momentary "relief" from the nagging feelings of withdrawal from alcohol.

It's like the "pleasure" you get when you take off a pair of tight shoes at the end of the day. Would you deliberately wear tight shoes just to get the relief of taking them off?

SO WHAT IF IT IS FAKE, AS LONG AS IT FEELS LIKE PLEASURE?

Some addicts, while they get this point without any problem, ask whether it really matters that the "pleasure" is fake. If it "feels" like pleasure, they say, isn't that the same?

The fact is, as all addicts know, the fake highs are not genuinely enjoyable, and they always leave you feeling worse. Once you understand how these fake highs work, even the illusion of pleasure evaporates.

GETTING CONNED

Consider this scenario. You make a new friend, who tells you they've had a successful week at work and want to celebrate with you with a few drinks after work in a swanky bar. They insist that it's their treat, waving off your protestations, so you go along with it. It's obviously what they want from the evening, and it's handy because you're a little low on cash at the moment.

So you have a great evening drink with them. The bar is fantastic, the drinks are tasty, the vibe is amazing, and it doesn't cost you a penny. You go home on a high. At the back of your mind, though, you know your friend must have spent $50 on drinks, and you won't feel totally comfortable until you've repaid the treat.

A week later, the same friend messages you, inviting you out after work again. It's exactly the same story: they've had an amazing week at work and they really want to share their success with you. Once again, they insist on picking up the tab. You don't want to spoil their mood so you go along with it and have another wonderful evening—a welcome release from the pressure you're under and the drudgery of staying in and saving your money.

You feel privileged by your friend's generosity, and you tell yourself that they seemed so happy to treat you, so excited and carefree, that it's really not worth worrying about returning the favor. If $50 a night is nothing to them, who are you to be a party pooper?

Another week passes and the same thing happens again: the invitation, the carefree hour or two, drinks with a fun friend who picks up the tab, and it's a wonderful release from your tight budget, especially since your bank account is emptier than ever. This goes on for a month or two, and you feel increasingly grateful for and flattered by your friend's generosity, and the fact that they want to share it with you.

But your own money worries keep getting worse, and you finally get around to checking your bank balance to see where else you can cut back. To your horror, you notice regular withdrawals of $100 that correspond with your after-work drinks! You feel sick, deeply shocked, and gradually your panic turns to anger as you realize that you've been conned.

It wasn't *them* buying the drinks—it was you!

Somehow your new so-called "friend" has gotten access to your bank account, taken out $100 every week, spent half of it on you and enjoyed themself on the rest. This person you thought was becoming your best friend is nothing of the kind. In fact, they are a thief. The worst kind of thief: one who fools you by making you think you're special, then rips you off behind your back.

Put yourself in that position. Having unveiled the truth, how would you feel about those after-work drinks now? Would you describe the way they made you feel as a genuine high? That's what it felt like at the time but now, looking back, wouldn't it make you feel sick? Used? Betrayed?

The friend you thought was so generous, kind, fun, and a genuine benefit in your life—how would you feel about them now? And how would you feel about yourself? At a time when money was tight, you allowed yourself to be ripped off. At some level, you would blame yourself. But you are not to blame. You're the victim.

This analogy perfectly describes your relationship with emotional drinking. Anything remotely positive that you felt you were experiencing from drinking was fake, phony, an illusion designed to trick you. Does it matter that the good times you think you had turned out to be fake? Damn right it does!

CHANGING YOUR MINDSET

If the only reason you drink is to relieve the low caused by the alcohol withdrawal from the previous drink, it seems reasonable to assume that all you need to do to break free is stop drinking. Put up with the withdrawal for the short time it takes for the drug to pass out of your body and the craving will stop.

We all know that this doesn't work, though. If it did, you would have quit by now without needing any help from me. The fly in the ointment is that, while it may begin with something you put in your body, addiction lives and grows in the mind.

We've known for a long time that people can be brainwashed by bombarding them with propaganda. Evil tyrants have used this technique with devastating effect throughout history. It's only recently, however, that we have begun to understand why we are susceptible to brainwashing.

Scientists have discovered that the brain is plastic, meaning it can be literally molded and remolded by conditioning. Think of it as a network of electrical connections that fire off every time we have a thought, process information, or pull something out of our memory. This network changes shape in order to give more capacity where it is needed and less where it is not.

If we are given a large amount of information on a particular subject, the network will remold itself to accommodate this information. This is how people become experts in specific fields; it's also how we become addicted. The brain's plasticity determines not only knowledge, but also attitude. We call it mindset. The brainwashing we are bombarded with about booze is designed to give us the mindset that drinking is fun, a pleasure, a comfort.

OUR TASK IS TO CORRECT THAT MINDSET.

It was understanding this aspect of addiction that enabled me to apply Easyway not only to smoking but also to alcohol addiction and other recognized addictions, like heroin addiction, as well as addictions that don't involve drugs, such as gambling and overeating. I don't mind admitting that I knew nothing about the workings of the brain when I discovered the method, but as I said before, it has been interesting to see science gradually confirm the basis of Easyway over subsequent years.

There are smokers who have quit but still crave cigarettes weeks, months, even years later. You probably know at least one. The same applies to people who quit alcohol. Some ex-drinkers go on craving alcohol for the rest of their lives. This is because they have quit through willpower; they haven't corrected their mindset, so they continue to live with the illusion that drinking gave them a pleasure or comfort, and they feel deprived without it.

We are brainwashed into believing that our "fix" is a source of pleasure or comfort, and those moments of partial relief from withdrawal reinforce the illusion. Thus we are deluded into thinking that happiness lies in the very thing that's causing us misery. Emotional drinkers are lured to alcohol by brainwashing. It is the illusion of pleasure that hooks you.

THE VOID AND ROLE MODELS

It's helpful at this stage if you can understand exactly why we are drawn to things that we know to be "bad for us." It would seem to go against the survival instinct that compels us to do things that are good for us. When we're brainwashed, as we are with regard to booze, our intellect overrides those survival instincts, convincing us that alcohol is a pleasure or comfort, *despite* the fact that it has a detrimental effect on our health.

The very fact that alcohol is "bad" is part of its appeal. We like the idea of being a bit naughty. It suggests personality, wit, nonconformity, individuality… it's an urge that is caused by an emptiness that opens up during our development, starting from birth. I call it "the void," and it affects all of us to different degrees.

From birth, as vulnerable infants, we desperately seek security and reach for our mothers for protection. Our neediness continues through childhood, when we're cocooned from the harsh realities of life in a world of make-believe. Sooner or later, though, we find out that Santa Claus and the Tooth Fairy don't exist.

At the same time, we're pushed from the safety of home into school, where we're exposed to a new set of fears and insecurities. As we enter adolescence, we start to look more critically at our parents and notice that they are not the unshakeable pillars of strength that we had always thought them to be. They have weaknesses, frailties, and fears, just as we do.

This realization opens up a void in our minds, a disillusioned feeling of emptiness and need. We fill the void with idols: rock stars, movie stars, celebrities, and athletes. We create our own fantasies. We idolize mere mortals and try to absorb some of their reflected glory. Instead of becoming complete, strong, secure, and unique individuals in our own right, we become followers, impressionable fans, leaving ourselves wide open to suggestion.

Faced with all this bewilderment and instability, we look for a little boost now and then. We've been brainwashed into believing that alcohol will give us the comfort and status we need, that it will make us feel relaxed and happy, that it will give us good times. So we naturally turn to drinking for relief from the void.

THE PITCHER PLANT

Have you ever seen a pitcher plant? It's a carnivorous plant, shaped like a slender jug, which catches flies with an ingenious and cruel confidence trick. The fly lands on the rim of the plant, attracted by the sweet smell of nectar. As it starts to feed, it doesn't realize that it is being lured further into the plant. The nectar is the very thing that is luring the fly to its death. The trap you are in is similar to a pitcher plant.

Before we start seeking comfort from alcohol, we're well aware of the dangers. We know that it can make us sick, delirious, overweight, loud, obnoxious, and out of control. It can end up costing us a fortune, and it can lead to severe chronic conditions like heart disease. We see homeless alcohol addicts on the street. But we also know that millions of people drink several times a week, apparently without suffering any health problems.

So we think we'll be OK; we'll be among the lucky ones. We think our bodies will be able to cope, and we don't expect to become addicted. Nobody starts off with that intention. So we set aside any concerns about the harmful effects of alcohol, tell ourselves we're in control and we can handle it, and focus on that mythical pleasure or comfort.

At the same time, we are constantly bombarded with enticements to drink. All those ad slogans, all those cool characters in movies and on TV, all those friends shouting it's their round, all those people drinking and laughing. They're all luring you into the trap.

So you take the plunge. You start drinking and, hey, nothing bad happens! So you drink again. But without making a conscious decision, you start to increase the quantity and frequency of your drinking. Just as heroin addicts increase the dose to get the same high, emotional drinkers increase their drinking.

YOU'RE ALREADY LOSING CONTROL.

In the early stages, you can con yourself that you're in control of when and how much you drink, and that there is no threat. But as time goes on and the pleasure or comfort you seek grows more and more elusive, you begin to sense that you're slipping further and further into a bottomless pit. It's an unhappy, insecure feeling that creates further anxiety and stress.

By now you've conditioned yourself to look for comfort from

bad feelings like anxiety and stress by drinking. So rather than dealing with the real cause of your misery, you use the temporary fix of emotional drinking.

You can see how this becomes a vicious circle of need, fix, withdrawal, need... and because you keep increasing the dose, the highs become more short-lived and the lows more intense; the net effect is an increasingly rapid descent, like the fly sliding into the belly of the pitcher plant.

This is how the trap works. It's how any addiction works.

EMOTIONAL DRINKERS SEEK COMFORT IN THE VERY THING THAT'S CAUSING THEM MISERY.

NATURE'S WARNING LIGHT

Pain serves a useful purpose; whether physical or emotional, it tells us that something is wrong. The natural solution is to identify the cause of the problem and fix it, but we're conditioned by modern medicine to take a different approach. We treat the symptoms, not the cause. Got a headache? Take a painkiller. Feeling anxious? Pop a Xanax.

If you're driving a car and the oil light comes on, what do you do? Put tape over the warning indicator? Or pull over and top up the oil? Both actions will stop the oil light from coming on, but only one will prevent the engine from seizing up.

THE DIFFERENCE BETWEEN YOU AND THE FLY

As you descend into the trap and begin to realize that you're losing control of your drinking, you notice that the physical effects are starting to show. You're gaining weight, or fighting harder and harder to avoid doing so, your skin is losing its glow, your hair is lank, you're getting out of breath more quickly. Friday night drinks turn into Thursday night drinks and, ultimately, become daily "wine o'clock" drinks. You try to cover up these signs and pretend they're not there, but they cast a dark shadow at the back of your mind. And as you slip further and further into the trap, they loom larger and larger, adding more and more to your misery.

You get into the futile cycle of trying to cut down, to deny yourself, then relieving the misery of deprivation by bingeing. Like the fly in the pitcher plant, you only realize you're trapped when you're well and truly hooked. But there is one crucial difference between the pitcher plant and the emotional drinking trap:

IT'S NEVER TOO LATE TO ESCAPE FROM THE EMOTIONAL DRINKING TRAP.

The trap you're in is not physical. Unlike the fly, you are not standing on a slippery slope. The trap is entirely mental. It's ingenious because it makes you your own jailer, so the more you struggle, the tighter the bonds become. Fortunately, that is also its fatal weakness. Because you are the one keeping yourself trapped, you are also the one with the power to set yourself free. All you have to do is follow the instructions in this book.

The wonderful thing is that when you stop, you will recover completely. Without the mental and physical lows induced by emotional drinking, you will be able to get back to a level of genuine normality, with genuine pleasures and the occasional natural low. You will start accepting these occasional lows as a natural part of life, not something you need to try to escape from with booze.

And remember that, while it's you who has the power to set yourself free, the fact that you've fallen into the trap has nothing to do with a flaw in your character or personality. Tens of millions of people, who have found themselves in the same trap and been convinced that they will never be able to escape, have broken free—and so will you.

DEBILITATING MYTHS

There are three major myths keeping you in the trap:

1. That alcohol gives you pleasure and comfort;

2. That quitting will be hard and miserable;

3. That you will miss drinking for the rest of your life.

If you continue to believe these three common myths, you will find it hard to quit. No matter how desperately you *want* to quit, part of your brain will tell you that you'll be happier if you don't. You need to change your mindset. You need to unravel these myths.

We are all conned into believing that alcohol gives pleasure and comfort. Even people who don't drink are brainwashed into believing that, to a certain extent. There is no genuine pleasure or comfort to be gained from emotional drinking. There is plenty of misery and discomfort, as you've discovered.

But part of your brain will still be telling you that drinking is a source of comfort for you, and you might be thinking, "Does it matter that it isn't true, if it feels like it is?"

There are two very strong arguments that should answer that question once and for all.

1. Emotional drinking is a threat to your physical and mental health, and if you keep burying your head in the sand, these grim realities will take a heavy toll.

2. If you were happy about your emotional drinking, you wouldn't be reading this book.

Eventually, all addicts realize that there is no pleasure or comfort in their addiction. By this stage they are like the fly descending rapidly into the belly of the pitcher plant. There is a point at which the fly senses that all is not well and thinks about flying out. It's almost always too late. The fly struggles a bit, loses its footing, and falls into the digestive juices.

For you, though, it's different. There is no physical force holding you back. So when you sense that you are being consumed by emotional drinking and want to break free, you are in a very strong position to do so. You know there is no pleasure, no comfort, no reason at all to keep drinking. From this strong foundation it is a short step to establishing the mindset you need to walk free.

The illusion of pleasure makes it harder for people to change their mindset. Once the illusion of pleasure is gone, there is only one thing holding you back, and that is fear.

It's an odd kind of fear—the fear that escaping from a miserable situation will leave you feeling even more miserable—but it's a genuine fear and we will tackle it very soon. But first we need to look more closely at the illusion of pleasure and the myths that keep it controlling your mind.

Chapter 6

ILLUSIONS

IN THIS CHAPTER

•*INSTINCT VERSUS INTELLECT* •*HOW TO IDENTIFY THE TRUTH*
•*I ENJOY THE TASTE* •*IT MAKES ME HAPPY*
•*I CAN HANDLE IT* •*IT'S THE WAY I'M MADE*

People who don't have an alcohol problem find it hard to understand why drinkers can't just stop. What they don't appreciate is that the trap is a web of illusions that make it impossible to see the way out. Easyway helps you see through those illusions, and thus enables your escape.

Emotional drinkers suffer from many negative feelings. Among them is a feeling of foolishness: "How can I be so stupid as to keep drinking when I know it's making me miserable?" It does seem incredible that a creature as intelligent and complex as a human being can be so easily conned into self-destruction. Remember, it's not just you who have been taken in; hundreds of millions of people have fallen for the same confidence trick.

In Chapter 2, I mentioned that the crucial difference between humans and wild animals is that animals survive solely by instinct. Humans also use instinct to survive—it tells us when and what to eat, it alerts us to danger, it even helps us find a mate—but we don't rely on instinct alone. We use our intellect to give us power over nature and the whole animal kingdom.

INTELLECT VERSUS INSTINCT

It's our intellect that has enabled us to learn and pass on our learning, and that has made us develop into a highly sophisticated species that is not only capable of building fantastic structures and machines, but also has an appreciation of art, music, romance, spirituality, and so on.

Intellect is a wonderful thing, but it can go to your head; we tend to respect intellectual behavior above instinctive behavior, and this is what has led us astray. Instinct is nature's survival kit, but when it conflicts with our intellect, we usually take the intellectual option.

WE THINK WE CAN OUTSMART
THE SURVIVAL INSTINCT.

A telling example is the athlete who needs a pain-killing injection in order to play. Their instincts are giving the clear signal to rest and allow the injury to heal, but their intellect tells them they can numb the pain and keep playing. The result is often irreversible damage to their body. Their instinct was right, but they chose to side with their intellect.

If you re-evaluate the "advances" the human race has made, you'll see that, rather than building on the advantage that nature has given us, we have devoted a remarkable amount of time to self-destruction. We have devised, and continue to devise, ever more sophisticated ways of killing each other. But it's not just when we're trying to be destructive that our intellect leads us astray. It's also evident when we're supposedly having fun.

We have become a species vulnerable to alcohol addiction by allowing our intellect to trick our instincts. We instinctively know that booze is bad for us, but intellectually we believe it works wonders for our happiness and social standing. So we drink despite our instincts, and the trap replaces genuine pleasures with the illusion of pleasure. We have created a substance that fools our instincts into thinking we are getting something good when, in truth, it is nothing but bad.

Be absolutely clear: there is NO BENEFIT WHATSOEVER IN DRINKING ALCOHOL.

There are many intellectual choices we make in life that are beneficial. For example, intellect enables us to forecast and pre-empt problems in a way that other animals can't, and thus better protect ourselves. But choosing to drink alcohol is not beneficial. So why make that choice?

The reason is:

WE DON'T ALWAYS REALIZE WE HAVE AN OPTION.

Drinking alcohol is a choice, of course. Nobody is holding a gun to your head and forcing you to drink. But the brainwashing is so strong, and the illusions it creates so convincing, that it sometimes doesn't occur to you that you have a choice.

There are a lot of people who stand to gain from the con. The brewers and distillers, the retailers, the marketeers... it is in their interests to find ways to convince you to make that decision. They target you from a young age and they have become masters at it. Your intellect is their greatest asset; it allows them to fill your head with false information that overrides your instincts and fools you into believing the three myths:

1. That drinking alcohol gives you pleasure and comfort;

2. That quitting is hard and miserable;

3. That the craving never goes.

HOW TO IDENTIFY THE TRUTH

It's not hard to trick the human mind. Remember the illusion with the three figures in Chapter 2? This is a visual example of how easy it is to plant false information in your mind. It also demonstrates the fact that once you've seen through an illusion, you can't be fooled by it again.

This helps answer a question that a lot of people ask of Easyway:

HOW DO I KNOW THAT EASYWAY IS NOT JUST BRAINWASHING ME IN A DIFFERENT WAY?

Addictions work by bombarding your mental process with a false sense of pleasure and reward, which your mind mistakes for the real thing. Your instinct is reprogrammed into believing that you need to drink alcohol in order to get the pleasure or comfort you need. At the same time, your intellect has been fed the same misinformation. As long as you continue to believe intellectually that alcohol gives you pleasure or comfort, you will not be able to reconnect with your instinct to distinguish this false reward from the real thing.

Easyway actually does the opposite of brainwashing. It helps you see through the illusions and unravel the myths that keep you in the trap. Rather than brainwashing, Easyway is counter-brainwashing.

The first illusion is the one that most of us are taken in by: that there is apparent enjoyment in the taste.

I ENJOY THE TASTE

From an early age, we are led to believe that there is something special about booze. As children, we're not allowed to have it, which gives it a mystique. We see our parents and their friends drink it at parties, then we see our heroes drink it on TV and in movies. By the time we are old enough to be allowed our first taste, we can't wait for this incredible experience.

But it's not incredible at all, is it? That first taste is repulsive. How can anyone say they like this stuff? But they do. They go on and on about a great beer or a sophisticated wine that develops on the palate. Booze is portrayed as a taste sensation, and it's the biggest con ever. They're selling us a foul-tasting poison dressed up as something to savor.

Intellectually, we are so taken in by this con that we push through those repulsive first sips until we can drink a beer or down a glass of wine without wanting to throw up. And guess what? We start to develop a taste for it. Of course, what we've really done is override our sense of taste. In order to "enjoy" alcohol, we have to smother the taste, often resorting to diluting it with sickly sweet mixers.

As we continue to drink, we tell ourselves that we do so because we enjoy the taste. But it's not the taste that keeps us coming back for more, nor is it the taste that gives us the illusion of pleasure. It's the drug. It's our addiction to alcohol.

IT MAKES ME HAPPY

Even at their lowest ebb, some emotional drinkers continue to regard alcohol as the one thing that can make them happy. It never dawns on them that it is the chief cause of their misery and anxiety.

We are conned into believing that booze is the social lubricant that helps us have a good time, as if we can't enjoy one another's company without it. The con is perpetrated by both the alcohol industry *and* the people who supposedly have our best interests at heart: chiefly our parents. They drink at birthday parties, weddings, anniversaries, Christmas. The message is clear: booze equals happiness.

We are not only brainwashed into believing that booze helps make happy occasions happier; we are also led to believe that it can lift our spirits when we're lonely or depressed.

Think about social occasions where booze has apparently helped create a wonderful, carefree atmosphere. Wouldn't the atmosphere have been wonderful and carefree anyway? Isn't that the mood everyone is in at a wedding or party or Christmas? It's not the booze that makes the occasion, it's the occasion itself. The booze is just a prop. And on many occasions, it completely spoils the party.

What about times when you've been down or upset, and somebody has given you a drink to comfort you? Can a foul-tasting poison really give you comfort? If you have understood my explanation of addiction, you will know that the illusion of comfort is merely the relief of discomfort, which was caused by drinking in the first place.

All emotional drinkers know that turning to alcohol for comfort or happiness doesn't work. Whatever is causing you to feel unhappy, drinking a poison that offers no benefits at all will not help. All it will do is partially relieve the low caused by the previous drink. The cause of your sadness, loneliness, or anxiety remains, and the effects of drinking make it worse. The lows and self-loathing that come with emotional drinking will always leave you more unhappy.

Emotional drinkers convince themselves that they enjoy seeking oblivion from booze because the thought of not drinking is too awful to contemplate. They know in their hearts that they don't really enjoy it, but admitting that means admitting that they are not in control and continue to drink only because they cannot stop.

You have a choice. Accept the obvious and follow the instructions to escape, or keep on kidding yourself to protect yourself from confronting the brutal truth: that emotional drinking is causing you immense physical and mental harm, which will eventually destroy you.

TAKE YOUR HEAD OUT OF THE SAND!

The reason you believe you get some pleasure or comfort from alcohol is because when you are not drinking, you feel restless, uncomfortable, and deprived. When you drink, the uncomfortable feeling is partially relieved as the feeling of deprivation is temporarily eased. We never attain full relief. How can we? Alcohol debilitates you both physically and mentally, and, as you go through life, your wellbeing is constantly declining; the lows get lower and the "highs" also decline in proportion. It feels like a boost when you have a drink, but it is only making you feel the way a non-addict feels all the time. It is not a genuine pleasure.

IT IS LIKE DELIBERATELY WEARING TIGHT SHOES JUST FOR THE PLEASURE OF TAKING THEM OFF!

I CAN HANDLE IT

Aside from the fact that this is a bizarre reason for choosing to do anything, all the evidence points to the fact that you can't handle it.

Along with the brainwashing, we are also warned from an early age that booze is harmful (usually with the caveat "if consumed in excess"). We know the damage it can do, but we grow up thinking we'll be ok; we won't be the ones with liver damage or heart disease. In fact, the thought that we might doesn't even occur to us. No one mentions the psychological misery of alcohol addiction and how it can creep up on anybody.

We see booze as a guilty pleasure, but nothing more sinister than that. You know for yourself how it can ensnare you in its trap and keep you hooked, even though you really wish you could stop. By the time you realize the real danger of alcohol, it's too late and you're already in the trap.

The good news is that it's never too late to escape. Once you've seen the truth, it's easy to dispel the illusion that drinking alcohol is a relatively harmless "habit."

IT'S THE WAY I'M MADE

Addicts of all kinds often blame their addiction on a flaw in their personality. It's either a weakness in their temperament—a lack of willpower—or a predisposition to addiction—an addictive personality. The conclusion in both cases is that the situation is beyond their control, and that's an excuse that suits addicts very well, because it removes the pressure to stop.

Soon I'll dispel the addictive personality myth. It cons us into making absurd decisions and behaving in absurd ways. Emotional drinkers know that their addiction is destructive, and desperately wish they could quit, but they lie and make excuses and try every deceit in the book to make sure they can continue to drink.

The trouble is that most of the information we are given about addiction states that you *do* need willpower to quit, and that there *is* such a thing as an addictive personality. The fact that this misinformation is pushed by many reputable organizations that exist to help addicts just adds to its power. Why would an organization that genuinely wants to help people put out information that serves to imprison them more deeply in the trap? The simple answer is because they, too, have been brainwashed by myths, illusions, and misunderstanding.

The absurdity of addiction is the reason why it's so important to have an open mind and follow the instructions. The truth is often the opposite of what we assume to be true.

Blaming your emotional drinking problem on a flaw in your personality is a form of denial. Instead of accepting that you have an addiction, and taking the necessary steps to overcome that addiction, it allows you to say, "I have no choice but to keep doing it." There is a peculiar comfort in claiming victim status that keeps people enslaved.

Why, you may ask, would anyone want to live like that? Why would anyone who is suffering from the misery and slavery of emotional drinking make an excuse that took away their option to walk free?

The answer can be encapsulated in one word. It's a word that lies at the root of all addictions:

FEAR.

Chapter 7

FEAR

Fear of the consequences of emotional drinking is the driving force that makes you want to quit, but there are other fears pulling you in the opposite direction. Let's help you dispel all your fears.

Addicts are renowned for making excuses. Emotional drinkers have to make excuses because they know there is no logical reason to keep turning to alcohol. Typical excuses are:

"I'm not feeling very strong today. Tomorrow will be different."

"I've already drunk most of the bottle; I might as well finish it."

You need excuses to keep being a slave to alcohol because you have a fear of what life might be like if you try to quit. You have been brainwashed into thinking that you derive some pleasure or comfort from drinking, so the thought of life without it is terrifying. But you're also very aware of the harm you're inflicting on yourself, and you're afraid of the long-term damage that might cause, not to mention the embarrassment and shame we increasingly feel as a result of our behavior or sense of feeling trapped. You're caught in a tug-of-war between conflicting fears, and it makes you think contradictory and illogical thoughts:

"I know it's making me miserable, but it's my one pleasure in life."

SOMETHING THAT MAKES YOU MISERABLE CANNOT BE A PLEASURE.

PROJECTED FEARS

We tend to hide our fears away, but fear is not something to be ashamed of. It's an incredibly powerful and vital emotion. Interestingly, fear can be both instinctive and intellectual. Instinctive fear is what drives us to fight or flight when we're threatened—a crucial survival mechanism.

Things that threaten and scare us can also be both real and imaginary. For example, a horror movie is not a real threat; there is no real danger. But the suggestion of danger is enough to trigger the instinct of fear.

Humans have the power to imagine danger even when there is none. This is both an asset and a handicap. It helps us learn to cross the street safely. It also helps us behave in ways that safeguard our future. You might fear losing your job. That's an intellectual fear. There is no danger as such, but you project the consequences that losing your job could entail, such as having no money, being forced to sell your possessions, losing your home, or even just sacrificing the pleasures and comforts that you enjoy now—that instils fear. So you do everything in your power to safeguard your job and make yourself indispensable, even when there is no present threat of losing your job.

Intellectual fear is helping you in this case, but it can become an unhealthy burden. If that projected fear gets out of hand, it can make you permanently anxious when there is nothing actually threatening you. The human ability to project can make you afraid of threats that don't exist AND NEVER WILL. Like the projected misery of life without alcohol.

You have absolutely nothing to fear from NOT drinking booze. You know very well that your health will improve, but you've been brainwashed into believing that some aspect of life without alcohol will be uncomfortable and miserable. We are all bombarded with so much false information that it's impossible to know what to believe until you test it. Consequently, we end up spending a lot of our life worrying about things that will never happen—and not worrying about things that will.

Fear is the basis of all addiction. It is the force that keeps you in the trap, afraid to take the simple steps that lead to your escape. It is ingenious because it works in reverse: it's when you're NOT drinking that you suffer the empty, insecure feeling that triggers the fear. When you do drink, you feel a small boost, which partially relieves the insecure feeling, and your brain is fooled into believing that drinking is providing a comfort.

This is why, as long as you remain an emotional drinker, you cannot find true happiness. When you're drinking, you wish you didn't have to. When you can't drink, you wish you could.

ONCE YOU UNDERSTAND THE TRAP COMPLETELY, YOU WILL HAVE NO NEED OR DESIRE TO DRINK ALCOHOL.

FEAR OF FAILURE

Being an emotional drinker is similar to being in prison. Whether your emotions seem to lead you to drink daily or binge infrequently, you're either resisting the urge to drink more or giving in to that urge. Every aspect of your life is controlled by drinking: your daily routine, your hopes, your view of the world, your suffering. You're not physically imprisoned, of course. There are no walls or bars. The prison is purely in your mind. But as long as you remain a slave to alcohol, you will experience the same psychological symptoms as an inmate in a real prison.

If you've tried and failed to quit, you know that failure makes you feel more firmly trapped and helpless than you did before you tried. I liken it to that moment in a movie when a prisoner is thrown into a cell and the first thing he does is run to the door and pull on the handle. This confirms his predicament: he really is locked in.

Trying and failing to quit reinforces the belief that you are trapped in a prison from which there is no escape. This can be a hugely dispiriting experience, and enough to keep you from trying again. You tell yourself that the best way to avoid the misery of failure is to avoid trying to quit in the first place. And as long as you never try to escape, you will always be able to preserve the belief that escape is possible. That's the twisted logic of addiction, and it can keep you well and truly trapped.

It's only when you try to escape that you fail, so it's best not to try. When it's written down like this, you can see how absurd addictive thinking is; but it's not so clear when you're the one caught in the trap. The belief that escape is possible is vital to an addict. It represents hope. Who wants to risk shattering their own hope?

There are millions of people around the world who continue to keep themselves trapped in this way. Intelligent, sensible people, who continue suffering the misery of addiction rather than risk the misery of failure. What they don't realize—and it's never pointed out to them until they discover Easyway—is that the person who pulls on the prison door and finds it firmly locked is using the wrong method of escape.

Tugging at the door is what you do when you use the willpower method. The trap is like a snare, which tightens its grip the more you struggle. That's why it's often people with very strong willpower who find it hardest to quit until they try Easyway.

Trying and failing to quit can be a crushing experience, but the fear of failure is illogical, because the thing you're fearing has already happened. You've become addicted. What could be worse? Every time you drink, you experience a sense of failure. As long as you remain an addict, you will continue to feel like a failure.

Fear of failure can be a positive force if it's channeled correctly. A runner on the starting blocks, a ballet dancer waiting in the wings, a student going into an exam; fear of failure is the little voice in their head that reminds them to prepare thoroughly, to remember everything they've rehearsed and trained for, and to leave nothing to chance. It can bring a remarkable clarity of thought and judgment.

But the addict's fear of failure is different, because it is based on an illusion, and it paralyzes the addict to the point of inaction. The simple truth is that you have nothing to lose by trying, even if you do fail. The worst that can happen is that you remain in the trap. By not trying, you guarantee that outcome. In other words:

> ### *IF YOU SUCCUMB TO THE FEAR OF FAILURE, YOU ARE GUARANTEED TO SUFFER THE VERY THING YOU FEAR.*

There is another fear we need to dispense with before you can escape and that is the fear of succeeding.

FEAR OF SUCCESS

Studies have shown that there is a common tendency for ex-prisoners to reoffend within a very short time of being released. It's easy to assume that these must be habitual criminals who know no other way of making a living, but research has found that, in fact, many ex-cons reoffend deliberately because they want to get caught. They actually *want* to go back inside.

Prison life is grim, but if it's the life they're used to it can be more attractive than the alternative... or less frightening, anyway. Life on the outside is unfamiliar and unnerving. They don't feel equipped to handle it. They yearn for the "security" of the prison. Addicts have a similar psychology. They become afraid that life without their "crutch" will feel alien and disconcerting; they won't be able to enjoy life or deal with its stresses; they might even have to go through some terrible trauma to break free, and then they'll be condemned to a life of sacrifice and deprivation.

When you've been brainwashed into believing that alcohol is a social lubricant and a source of fun, it's natural to fear that life without it will be dull. For emotional drinkers, this fear becomes the monster that keeps you in the trap. Although you're well aware that your drinking is no fun at all, you might still see it as part of your identity. Perhaps you've even convinced yourself that people like you for it.

We see it all the time in the media: the boozer who doesn't seem to care, who isn't tied down by those petty concerns that make everyone else so uptight and boring. They're portrayed as being more fun, more exciting, more attractive. Maybe you believe this portrayal. Perhaps you believe that this person is you. But ask yourself:

Do you feel exciting?

Do you feel lovable?

Are you really having fun?

Let's be absolutely clear about this: you have nothing to lose by escaping from the emotional drinking trap. Life without the slavery of addiction is not something to fear; it is something to look forward to with excitement and elation. If you choose to stay in the trap, you will feel like a failure for the rest of your life. This is NOT the life you were born for. You DO have a choice.

WIN THE TUG-OF-WAR

The trap makes you your own jailer. That is both its fiendish ingenuity and its fatal flaw. The panicky feeling that makes you afraid to even try to quit drinking is caused by drinking. One of the greatest benefits you'll receive when you quit is never to suffer that fear again.

The tug-of-war is a conflict between two fears: the fear of what emotional drinking is doing to you and the fear of life without your little "crutch." One of these fears is valid because it's based on fact; the other is invalid because it's based on illusions. The tug-of-war is easy to win, because both fears are caused by the same thing: alcohol.

TAKE AWAY THE BOOZE AND THE FEAR GOES TOO.

I wish I could transport you forward into your mind and body, to the time when you finish reading this book. You would think, "Wow! Will I really feel this good?" Fear will have been replaced by elation, the feeling of failure by optimism, self-loathing by confidence, apathy by dynamism. All these psychological turnarounds will benefit your physical health, too. You will look fitter and fresher, and you'll enjoy both a newfound energy and the ability to truly relax.

Some people manage to go for weeks, months, even years without succumbing to the temptation to drink, but still find that they miss it. You may have been through this yourself. Quitting with Easyway is different. You will not miss it, because you are not giving anything up. There is no sacrifice involved because alcohol does nothing for you whatsoever.

All you are doing is getting rid of something in your life that makes you miserable, leaving you with a sense of release, freedom, and beautiful calm. It's no more complicated than throwing away a pair of horribly uncomfortable, tight shoes and replacing them with a comfortable new pair.

YOU ARE NOT GIVING ANYTHING UP.

You are making a simple and logical trade: lack of control over your drinking for total control; no choice for absolute choice.

Right now, part of you believes that alcohol is your friend, your constant companion, and comfort. Get it clearly into your mind that this is an illusion. In reality, alcohol is your worst enemy and, far from supporting you, it's driving you deeper and deeper into misery. You instinctively know this, so open your mind and follow your instincts.

REMOVE ALL DOUBTS

Think about all the wonderful things you stand to gain by overcoming your emotional drinking. Take a moment and think about the enormous self-respect you'll regain, and the time and energy you'll save by not having to make excuses and cover up your drinking.

That phony little boost you think you get from your fix of alcohol is a mere hint of how you will feel all the time when you're free. Escape from the control and slavery, from the anxiety, shame, and perpetual remorse is priceless.

WHEN YOU'RE FREE, IT'S REAL.

If only addicts could step outside their world and see their problem as other people see it. But addiction makes it very hard, if not impossible, to do that. If you saw a heroin addict suffering the misery of drug addiction, would you advise them to keep injecting heroin into their veins? If you can see that the heroin addict's "high" is nothing more than temporary relief from the discomfort caused by the drug as it leaves the body, and the cravings caused by the addict's mistaken belief that the drug provides them with a genuine pleasure or benefit, you are well on your way to understanding your own addiction.

And it should be clear to you that there is only one way to remove your craving permanently.

STOP DRINKING!

As soon as you can see that there is nothing to fear, that you are not giving up anything or depriving yourself in any way, stopping becomes easy.

You've had three instructions so far, to put you in the right frame of mind to enable this book to help you overcome your emotional drinking problem:

1. Follow all the instructions.

2. Keep an open mind.

3. Begin with a feeling of elation.

If you are struggling with any of these instructions, go back and re-read the relevant chapters. It's essential that you not only follow the instructions, but also understand them.

Remember what we have established: alcohol does absolutely nothing positive for you whatsoever; the beliefs that have kept you in the trap are merely illusions; you have everything to gain and nothing to lose by quitting. So can we agree that there is absolutely nothing to fear? If so, you're ready to move on.

If you're afraid that the process of quitting itself will be unpleasant, perhaps because you've tried to quit before and found it difficult, remember that the willpower method makes it hard. It leaves you feeling deprived, which means you can never completely rid yourself of the desire to drink. The willpower method either doesn't work or leaves people trapped in a lifelong battle resisting the urge to drink on a daily basis.

True freedom is only attained if your desire to drink is removed, and that requires you to remove the fears of success and failure. You must be 100 percent certain about your desire to quit.

FOURTH INSTRUCTION: NEVER DOUBT YOUR DECISION TO QUIT.

As you continue through the book, you will be challenged to see things in a new way. This may cause you to have some doubts. It's fine to question what you read here, because that will help reinforce the logic and truth behind it. But if you find yourself doubting your decision to quit, remind yourself why you chose to read this book in the first place and think about all the wonderful gains you stand to make.

If you're absolutely sure about your desire to quit but not so sure about your ability to do so, that's probably because you're not yet convinced that it's possible to quit without willpower. It's time to address this particular myth once and for all.

Chapter 8

WILLPOWER

Willpower is a fine human characteristic. It gives us the resilience to push past obstacles and achieve all sorts of incredible feats. But addiction is not an obstacle to be pushed out of the way; it is a subtle, ingenious trap, and using willpower to try to overcome it is counterproductive. You just need to understand it. It is a classic case of "brains over brawn" and although one of the strengths of the trap is its simplicity, that is also its greatest weakness: anyone can understand it and escape from it.

Easyway can help you overcome emotional drinking without any discomfort or feeling of sacrifice. Therefore, you have no need for willpower. People often respond to this claim by saying, "If it's so easy, why do so many people find it incredibly hard?" The answer is simple: they are using the wrong method.

Even the simplest task can be made virtually impossible if you go about it the wrong way. Consider the simple act of opening a door. You push on the handle and it swings open with very little effort. But if you have ever come across a door with no handle and accidentally pushed on the wrong side, where the hinges are, you'll know that it puts up quite a fight. The door might budge a tiny bit but it won't swing open. You would need a huge amount of effort and determination to open it far enough for you to walk through.

Of course, you don't keep pushing on the wrong side; you change your method, push on the correct side, and the door opens so easily you barely notice it.

THE WRONG METHOD

Overcoming addiction is just like opening a door. Go about it the wrong way and it's incredibly hard; use the right method and it's a cinch.

The misconception that quitting addictions is hard exists because most addicts try to use willpower to overcome their desire. The emotional drinker's desire for alcohol is strong, so they have a constant conflict of will, a mental tug-of-war. Their rational brain knows they should stop because it's damaging their health, appearance, self-esteem, relationships, and happiness. But their addicted brain sends them into a panic at the thought of being deprived of what they perceive as their pleasure or comfort.

Anyone who tries to quit with the willpower method is setting themselves up for a series of setbacks. First you focus on all the reasons for stopping and hope your will is strong enough to hold out until the desire eventually disappears. This seems logical, but there's a problem: you still see booze as a pleasure or comfort. Therefore, when you stop drinking, you feel you're depriving yourself. This makes you miserable. It also makes you think you deserve a reward when you abstain for a period. And what do you do when you need to cheer up, or you deserve a reward? Drink!

THE WILLPOWER METHOD MAKES
YOU MORE HOOKED THAN EVER.

Relying on willpower to stop implies that you have a conflict of will. But we can resolve that conflict simply by removing one side of the tug-of-war, so that you have no desire for alcohol. Using willpower for the rest of your life to try not to drink is unlikely to succeed and will not make you happy; removing the desire to drink will.

I accept that some people do manage to stop their addictive behavior through sheer force of will. But do they ever actually break free of their addiction? There are people who quit for years and then fall back into the trap. We meet lots of them at Easyway when they finally seek our help. They've stayed dry for so long that their addiction is a distant memory, but they still believed that booze is a pleasure or comfort. They haven't removed the desire or the sense of sacrifice, and all it took was something to trigger their need for a pick-me-up or reward and they fell back into the clutches of their old fix. Their will fails and they find themselves back in the trap, feeling more miserable than ever.

DO YOU REALLY THINK YOU'RE WEAK-WILLED?

Because there is a general assumption that quitting requires willpower, there's also an assumption that those who fail to quit are weak-willed. We even think that about ourselves! If you think you've been unable to control your emotional drinking because you lack the willpower, you haven't yet understood the nature of the trap you're in.

The fact is that strong-willed people actually find it harder to quit. Why? Because they refuse to open their mind and accept that they're using the wrong method. They're stubborn. They would rather grapple with the problem than accept that they've been brainwashed and are not in control. And remember, the more you fight to get out of the trap, the more tightly ensnared you become.

TRYING AND FAILING TO QUIT IS MORE LIKELY TO BE A SIGN OF A STRONG WILL THAN A WEAK ONE.

AN ENDLESS STRUGGLE

So before you assume you can't quit because you lack the willpower, ask yourself whether you're weak-willed in other ways. Maybe you're a smoker or a gambler and you see these conditions as further evidence that you're weak-willed. Well, there is a connection between all addictions, but it's not that they are evidence of a lack of willpower. In fact, they are more likely to be signs of a strong will. What they all have in common is that they are mental traps created by misleading information and untruths—and one of the most misleading untruths is that quitting requires willpower, because when you think something is going to be hard and unpleasant, you find excuses not to try.

IN HER OWN WORDS: TERESA

"I was born with a disability that held me back in certain physical ways, but not mentally. On the contrary, I was a bright kid and I wanted the world to know it.

"Growing up, the thing that annoyed me most was being patronized. I didn't want anyone to treat me differently; I wanted to compete and succeed on my own merits. And I did. I sailed through my degree and received numerous job offers, but I didn't want to follow a well-trodden path. I wanted to do my own thing. So I set up my own software business and made sure it did really well.

"Part of wanting to be treated like everyone else was drinking like everyone else. Starting in my mid-teens, I was quite a big drinker. I was competitive about that, too. I didn't want anyone to think they could out-drink me!

"I didn't think it was a problem until I was in my late 20s, and I sold my business for a lot of money. Suddenly I found myself with time on my hands and plenty of money—a lethal combination for an alcoholic. I recognize now that that's what I was, although I would never have admitted it at the time.

"Anyway, it got pretty bad, to the point where I had a fall. And that led to a severe health scare. It scared me, and I told myself I had to quit boozing. I had been drinking to fill the hours, the loneliness, the boredom. It wasn't making me happy; it was bringing me down, so I made up my mind to kick it.

"I'm a determined girl, so I got into quitting with the same resolve that I had applied to my studies and my business. But this felt different. Things weren't falling into place the way they used to. It was a real struggle. It felt like I was fighting against myself, rather than against a feeble drug. But I dug in, because that's what I always did, and I managed to stay dry for a year. When I woke up that morning after exactly one year without booze (yes, I had been counting the days), I punched the air and congratulated myself, but my first feeling was, 'You can have a drink tonight, Teresa. You've earned it.'

"I managed to wait until the evening, and then I had a drink with dinner. Within a week, I was drinking every day."

You know that alcohol is damaging your mind and body, sabotaging your performance at work, your behavior toward others, and making you feel weak-willed and helpless. But you keep finding excuses to do it. That is not the behavior of a weak-willed person. It takes a strong will to persist in doing something that goes against all your instincts.

Emotional drinkers go to great lengths to cover up their addiction: sneaking out after dark to buy booze, hiding how much they're drinking, lying to friends and family... all these acts take a lot of planning and determination.

If you tried to open a door by pushing on the hinges and, despite being advised to push on the other side, you continued to push on the wrong side, I'd call you willful, not weak-willed. The prisoner who reoffends soon after being released from prison is not weak-willed; he is displaying a strong will to get back inside.

Consider for a moment anyone you know who has a drinking problem. It's probably a small number, because most people don't like to admit it. Let's also think of some high-profile examples. There have been plenty over the years to prove that alcohol addiction is not exclusive to the weak-willed.

Political leaders, movie stars, professional athletes, doctors, scientists... the list is long. Do you think all of these people lacked willpower? Did they get to the top without needing determination? Of course not.

Now ask the same question of yourself: are you really weak-willed? I'm sure you can find plenty of evidence to show that you are strong-willed. How do you react when people tell you you shouldn't have another drink? Do you tend to do the opposite? Wouldn't you describe that as willful?

When strong-willed people try to quit with the willpower method, they tend to find it harder than anyone else, because when the door fails to open, they won't give up and try to find an easier method. They'll force themselves to keep pushing on the hinges until they can push no more.

IN HIS OWN WORDS: CRAIG

"Where I come from, you start drinking at an early age. So by the time I was 30, I was pretty much pickled. And then my dad died. He was 55 years old but he looked about 80. It shook me up. I was considered a tough guy in my neighborhood, and nothing ever frightened me until I saw my dad in that hospital bed, struggling to stay alive. I realized I was heading the same way, and I wasn't happy about it. I had two kids, and I wanted to see them grow up. So I swore I would get off the booze.

"I went five years, but I would say that every day was murder. I couldn't go near a liquor store. I had to keep away from the liquor aisle in the grocery store. I couldn't walk past a bar, and I couldn't have booze in the house. It felt like every waking hour was a study in concentration, just trying to get my mind off of alcohol.

"I stopped seeing my friends, stopped going to other people's houses, and avoided any possibility of being around booze. It wasn't much of a life, to be honest, but I had made my mind up and I was going to stick to it. That's the kind of person I am: when I tell myself I'm going to do something, I do it.

"Five years... and then my mom died. It was the last straw. I felt like I deserved a reward for all my efforts, but all I got was grief. It was like believing in God and living like a monk, and then you decide there is no God. I was shattered. I couldn't go another day. I remember the first drink I had after five years. It was like I'd never been away. All the hard work, all the determination, it all faded to nothing in a moment and there I was, drinking again, getting drunk again.

"You'd think I'd lose the taste for it after five years. But no—I wanted that drink as much as any drink I had had in my entire life. But it floored me. All that effort for nothing. I was furious with myself. I kept saying to myself, 'You were so close! Just a little bit longer, and you'd have been free of it!' But looking back years later, after Easyway helped me quit for good, I don't think I was anywhere near the finish line. I fought with all my strength to resist booze, but that burning desire for a drink never left me. In fact, the more I fought, the stronger the desire became."

Craig is right. When you try to quit with the willpower method, you never reach the finish line. The struggle never ends. As long as you continue to believe that you're giving something up, you will always be running in pain. The more strong-willed you are, the longer you will withstand the agony. Craig had the strength to hold out for five years, but his pain never went away; it only got worse. The longer he felt deprived, the more powerful his craving became.

CROSSING THE LINE

When you quit with Easyway, there is a finish line, and you don't have to wait to cross it. With Easyway, you cross the finish line as soon as you remove the fear and illusions and lose the desire for alcohol. That's when you are free of the addiction that turned you into an emotional drinker. You need to understand that you will not get to that line by forcing yourself to suffer.

We've helped tens of millions of addicts, and I know first-hand that they do not respond well to a hardline approach like the willpower method. Instead of helping you quit, it actually encourages you to stay hooked because:

1) It reinforces the myth that quitting is hard, and therefore adds to your fear.

2) It creates a feeling of deprivation, which you will try to alleviate in your usual way—you will fall back into the trap.

If you have tried and failed using the willpower method, you know it's even harder to try again, because you have reinforced the belief that your problem is impossible to solve.

People like Craig will testify to an enormous sense of relief when they first give in after trying to quit with the willpower method. It's important to recognize that this relief is just a temporary end to the self-inflicted pain. It's not a relief that makes you feel happy. No one celebrates falling back into the trap. Craig woke up furious with himself. This is a common experience among emotional drinkers. Of course, in Craig's case, the relief wasn't due to ending withdrawal... he hadn't drunk alcohol in years. It was entirely down to what was going on in his mind.

That first drink after you've tried to quit is not pleasurable at all, despite what others might tell you. They're confusing pleasure with the relief of ending their pain. It's nothing more than the feeling of relief you get when you take off a pair of tight shoes at the end of the day. Imagine how that would feel after five years!

BEWARE OTHER QUITTERS

There always seems to be someone you know who is staying off of booze for a while and using willpower to do so. It's tempting to admire their resolve and wish you could do the same. Don't be fooled! Remember what you have learned about the willpower method and see things as they really are.

Other drinkers who try to quit with the willpower method can have a disruptive effect on your own desire to quit. They either brag about the sacrifices they're making, or complain about them. Either way, they reinforce the false belief that quitting means sacrifice.

Ignore the advice of anyone who claims to have quit with the willpower method.

THE TRUTH IS, THERE IS NO SACRIFICE.

The method you are following here is proven to work in freeing addicts from the misery of emotional drinking. It is a simple, logical method for unraveling the brainwashing and removing all desire for alcohol. It's important that you understand that you are not giving up anything. As soon as you can see this, you will end the tug-of-war. Without the tug-of-war, there is no need for willpower. Take away the fear and there is nothing to tug against. It's easy.

Craig was waiting for the day when he could stop fighting. But with Easyway there is nothing to wait for. As soon as you dispel the belief that alcohol gives you pleasure or comfort, you remove the desire and cure your addiction.

It's a genuine thrill, the moment you realize that you're no longer a slave. If you've followed all the instructions and understood everything you've read so far, you should already be feeling a thrilling sense of anticipation. You have taken a major step in solving your emotional drinking problem, and you can see where you're going.

You are in control, and soon you will be free. That said, if you remain unsure or nervous, please don't worry—just keep reading and following the instructions and you can't fail.

There's just one more possible hazard that could be holding you back from feeling like you're regaining control. Addicts who try to quit and fail blame it on a lack of willpower. You now know that's not the case. Addicts who try to quit and fail again and again blame it on something bigger, a flaw in their genetic makeup, commonly referred to as an "addictive personality."

No matter who you are, the only reason why anybody who tries to quit fails to quit is that they are using the wrong method. Until you take away the desire, you will never be free from the temptation that drags you back into the trap. You have given yourself the perfect opportunity to quit with the method that works—a method that has worked for countless addicts who have tried and failed many times with the willpower method.

So let's make sure you are not held back by any thoughts of a flaw in your personality.

Chapter 9

WHAT IF I HAVE AN ADDICTIVE PERSONALITY?

IN THIS CHAPTER

•A CONVENIENT EXCUSE •JUST ANOTHER MYTH
•SO WHY ME? •BORN VULNERABLE?
•THE STATISTICAL ARGUMENT

There is a theory that some people are more prone to addiction than most because of the way they're made, and if you happen to be one of them, there's not much you can do about it. The truth is, anyone can free themselves from emotional drinking simply by following the instructions of Easyway.

It's common for emotional drinkers to experience a feeling of foolishness and weakness whenever they find themselves drinking for comfort. The tug-of-war between wishing they could stop the damage and fearing what life would be like without alcohol creates a state of constant conflict, which is confusing, frustrating, and debilitating.

So you make excuses to overcome these unsettling feelings:

"I've worked hard all day; I deserve a drink."

"I've had a really bad week; I need a pick-me-up."

Emotional drinkers make these excuses on the false assumption that alcohol gives you some sort of pleasure or comfort, but the real purpose they serve is to explain away their inability to resist the urge to keep drinking.

When you understand how the trap works and how it controls you, you can no longer pretend there's any substance to these excuses, so you can't use them anymore. If you understand the fact that alcohol gives you nothing whatsoever—no pleasure, no comfort—then this is not a problem. You don't need excuses because there is no temptation.

For drinkers who still feel the pull of temptation despite knowing that their usual excuses have been dismantled, there's a compulsion to find another explanation: the addictive personality theory.

A CONVENIENT EXCUSE

The addictive personality theory assumes that some people are genetically programmed to pursue addictive behaviors. No matter how much they try to resist, there's something in the way they're made that turns them into addicts. It could be nicotine, it could be heroin, it could be alcohol; they will inevitably become hooked on something and once they are, they can't break free again. Their personality keeps them trapped.

Many addicts pounce on this theory because it's a convenient excuse to stay in the trap. The safety of the prison and the fear of quitting overwhelm their desire to become free, and the theory gives them an excuse to stop trying. This sounds miserable, and it is, but it appeals to them because:

- They believe their fix gives them pleasure or comfort.

- They think quitting is hard.

- They're afraid they won't be able to cope without their little crutch.

So what do you believe? If you still accept any of these myths, you need to go back and re-read Chapters 6 and 7. It is essential that you understand and have no doubt whatsoever that:

- Alcohol gives you no pleasure or comfort whatsoever; it just gives you partial relief from the craving caused by the previous drink.

- Quitting is easy when there is no conflict of will.

- Life without booze will leave you feeling amazing compared to how you feel now.

Falling back on the addictive personality theory will only guarantee that you remain in the trap forever; you will suffer more and more, and your misery will lead you closer and closer to despair.

JUST ANOTHER MYTH

The addictive personality theory was dreamed up by so-called addiction experts who noticed patterns among certain addicts that seemed to suggest a common trait. These patterns included:

- Craving a fix years after quitting;

- Getting hooked on multiple addictions;

- Getting much more seriously hooked than others;

- Sharing personality traits with other addicts.

But we know why some addicts continue to crave long after they've quit. Addiction is predominantly a mental condition, not a physical one, and if you stop drinking without removing the belief that alcohol gives you pleasure or comfort, you will always feel deprived and will always have to fight temptation.

The second pattern, multiple addictions, is fairly common, but it's not caused by an addictive personality. If you fall into the trap with one drug, why wouldn't you fall into the trap with all of them? It's the same trap, built on the same false belief that you're getting some sort of pleasure or comfort. Remember:

THE MISERY OF THE ADDICT IS NOT RELIEVED BY THE THING THEY ARE ADDICTED TO; IT'S CAUSED BY IT.

IN HIS OWN WORDS: BILL

"Like most of my friends, I started going to bars when I was in my teens and, along with drinking beer, I would smoke cigarettes. The two just went together. I didn't think there was anything wrong with it—most of us did it. It just felt like a way of life, and no one seemed to be suffering for it, probably because we were young and healthy.

"Fast forward 30 years, and I was still smoking and drinking, but I wasn't healthy any more. I'd stopped physical activity and started gaining weight. I thought smoking was supposed to keep you thin, but it clearly wasn't doing that for me. I had actually tried to quit smoking on several occasions, but I'd always come back to it. I hadn't tried to quit booze, because I didn't see that as so much of a problem. I should have, because every time I had a drink, I wanted a cigarette.

"The weird thing is that I regarded my beer and my cigarettes as two of my main pleasures in life, but I was also becoming aware that they were making me miserable. They didn't make me feel good; they made me feel like a failure, a slave. So why did I keep going back to them? I understood the drawbacks. Why wasn't that enough to make me quit? I heard about this addictive personality theory and thought, 'That must be me.' It was kind of comforting—it meant I didn't have to think about quitting any more, because there was no way I could.

"But then I got ahold of a copy of *The Easyway to Stop Drinking,* and there was Allen Carr telling me that my addiction was not my fault. I was in a trap, brainwashed by myths and tied up by illusions. It all started to make sense: the contradictions, the twisted logic, the desire to quit conflicting with the fear of being deprived.

"When I'd tried to quit smoking, I had substituted cigarettes with candy, and become hooked on candy. Whatever I turned to, I seemed to get addicted to it; that's why I assumed it was some flaw in my personality. Thanks to *Easyway,* I could see that I could quit smoking without any substitutes and, if I could quit smoking, I could quit drinking too. My mindset changed completely.

"I gave it a try and it worked. Within a month, I'd quit smoking and drinking, and I felt no desire for either, nor candy, nor any other substitutes. And I thought, 'If I can do it, anyone can.' So I started telling my friends. To date, there are five of us who no longer smoke or drink, and we agree that life has never been better."

SO WHY ME?

Some people fall deeper into the trap than others. Why should this be, if it's the same trap for everybody? Why can some people have the occasional drink, while others always get blotto? Doesn't that suggest that personality must play a part?

The way we behave is governed by all sorts of influences. As we grow up, we are all subjected to different conditions and role models: parents, teachers, friends, things we read, watch and listen to, places we go, people we meet, etc. These form part of the brainwashing, and they will have an influence on how quickly we fall into the trap. People with time and money on their hands, for example, tend to fall into the trap faster because there are fewer obstacles to hold them back.

If you believe that alcohol gives you pleasure or comfort, and every time you drink you feel the partial relief of the craving caused by the previous drink, then your belief will increase, your desire will increase, and your determination to drink more will increase.

IT IS THE BELIEF THAT ALCOHOL GIVES YOU PLEASURE OR COMFORT THAT SPEEDS UP YOUR DESCENT INTO THE TRAP.

BORN VULNERABLE?

Addicts often tell us that they feel like they're a different breed from everyone else. When they get together, they find that they share similar character traits: an unstable temperament, which swings between exuberance and misery; a tendency toward excess; a high susceptibility to stress, evasiveness, anxiety, and insecurity. They feel more comfortable in the company of other addicts. It's tempting to believe that these character traits are evidence of a shared personality flaw, which has doomed them all to be addicts. The reality is that these traits are the *result* of addiction.

Drinkers tend to feel more comfortable in the company of other drinkers, but not because they're more interesting, free-spirited, or fun. The mutual attraction lies in the very fact that they won't challenge one another or make each other think twice about their addiction. Why? Because they're all in the same boat.

All emotional drinkers know that they're doing something foolish and self-destructive, but if they surround themselves with other people who are doing the same thing, they don't feel so bad. The destructive emotions of weakness, helplessness, stupidity, and hopelessness are a terrible reality for all addicts. They are the main cause of misery, and they drive you back to your little crutch time and time again.

The good news is that once you're free of your addiction, you won't just be saved from the unhealthy physical effects of emotional drinking; you will also be liberated from the terrible impact it has on your psyche.

THE STATISTICAL ARGUMENT

The addictive personality theory is all about genetics. It assumes that there is a gene that makes some people predisposed to addiction. If that's the case, there should be a fairly consistent proportion of the world's population who are addicts, shouldn't there?

But this is not the case. Look at the statistics for smoking, which has undergone more research than any other addiction. In the 1940s, more than 80 percent of the UK adult male population smoked; today that figure is well under 20 percent. A similar trend is evident throughout most of the West. If the addictive personality theory is valid, that means that there has been a significant change in the genetics of 60 percent of the population in just over half a century. That's preposterous!

Meanwhile, as the number of smokers in the West has plummeted, the number in the East has soared. So what happened? Have all the people with addictive personalities migrated to Asia, and vice versa?

Emotional drinking and its related health risks are on the increase. But no one is chalking this up to an increase in addictive personalities; they're blaming the amount of cheap booze on the market, the influence of advertising, and a proliferation of negative role models. In the face of this brainwashing, you need to maintain a clear understanding of the trap they're trying to lure you into. Remember, when you've seen through an illusion, you cannot be fooled by it again.

Get it clear in your mind that you didn't become an emotional drinker because you have an addictive personality. If you think you do, it's simply because you got hooked. This is the trick that addiction plays on you. It makes you feel that you're dependent on alcohol, and that there's some vulnerability in your makeup. It distorts your perceptions and keeps you enslaved.

The addictive personality theory is bad news for addicts because it reinforces the belief that escape is impossible; therefore, there's no point trying. This is a myth created by the illusions that alcohol gives you pleasure or comfort, and that quitting is hard. See through the illusions, deconstruct the myths, and escape is easy.

As you continue to read this book, you will put the misery and slavery of emotional drinking behind you. Once you can see the situation as it really is, you'll wonder how you were ever conned into seeing it differently. You are one of millions of people around the world who have been the victim of an ingenious trap. Recognize the trap for what it is, dismiss the idea of a vulnerability in your personality or genetic makeup, and you will be ready to walk free.

Chapter 10

WHY WE GET HOOKED

IN THIS CHAPTER
•*THE BRAINWASHING BEGINS* •*FATAL ATTRACTION*
•*WHY WE KEEP DRINKING* •*TWO MONSTERS*
•*FACE YOUR FEAR* •*STAY RESOLUTE*

Now that we have established that your emotional drinking problem is not caused by a flaw in your DNA, nor a lack of willpower, but by a mixture of myths and illusions, you are ready to begin your escape. Let's start unraveling those illusions, beginning with the reason why you got hooked in the first place.

In Chapter 5, I talked about the psychological void that is created in us from birth, and makes us feel insecure and in need of comfort. The void is like an emptiness in your life that needs to be filled.

Everybody experiences the void to some extent, but it varies because everyone has different experiences as they grow up. Some of us feel more driven to fill the void than others. The most common time of life to do this is during our teens, when hormones are raging, parents are getting on our nerves, we're feeling pressure from school and trying to establish our place in society. It's a time of huge transition, disillusionment, and insecurity, and we feel like we need something to cling to. This is often the time of life when addictions begin.

We've been waiting to "come of age," and we're excited to find out what this "social lubricant" is all about. All our lives, we've been given the clear message that booze will make us happy. When you're given a message like that from the people you trust most, you naturally take it on board.

So we grow up believing that alcohol can give us pleasure or comfort. We also perceive it as a sign of being grown up. No wonder so many young people get heavily into drinking at such an early age, before it is legal for them to do so.

That process is facilitated by one of the most sophisticated marketing machines on the planet: the alcohol industry. New alcoholic beverages have been introduced to lure kids in. Bright, neon-colored "shot" drinks—sickly sweet to soften the initial "gag reflex" that hard liquor always used to provoke in kids. This process means that some remain slaves to it for life.

There are plenty of people, of course, who experience the same brainwashing but don't develop an emotional drinking problem. So how are they different from you?

Think of them as flies that haven't landed on the pitcher plant yet. They, too, believe that alcohol provides pleasure or comfort; they just haven't yet felt the need to try it for themselves. But all it takes is a crisis to shake them up emotionally, or maybe another addiction to overcome, and they, too, will fall into the trap.

In fact, there are plenty of people who develop an emotional drinking problem in their 30s or 40s, or even later. They have lived with the belief that alcohol could give them pleasure or comfort, but they have also been aware of the drawbacks; until now, their desire has never been enough to outweigh the drawbacks. But one trauma is enough to tip the balance.

FATAL ATTRACTION

When you feel sad or insecure, you look for things to cheer yourself up. That's perfectly natural and normal. But why do we believe that we will get that pleasure or comfort from things we know are harmful?

Although we grow up being told that alcohol gives pleasure and comfort, we are also told that it's not good for us. It is no secret. We grow up fully informed about the possible health impacts associated with alcohol, but we also grow up seeing our parents and other role models "enjoying" a drink. This makes us regard alcoholism as one of those things that happens to other people. We become complacent.

As humans, we tend to be attracted to things that we are warned about. Danger makes it even more enticing. Don't go into the haunted house! Don't lean over the railing! Don't stick your head out the window!... What's the first thing you do when your parents aren't looking?

BY WARNING US ABOUT ALCOHOL, SOCIETY INCREASES THE TEMPTATION TO TRY IT.

It's a classic case of intellect overriding instinct. We've been warned about drinking too much, but we've also been told it gives us pleasure and comfort. Then we see our role models drinking, so we suspect their warnings must be exaggerated.

"Sure, some people become dependent on alcohol, but there must be something fantastic about it to make all these people drink despite the danger."

"Sure, alcohol can cause obesity, liver damage, heart disease, and lots of other severe medical conditions, but it must make you feel great for so many people to take that chance."

Instead of taking the warnings at face value, we intellectually look for the hidden message: "If people are doing it in spite of all the dangers I've been warned about, there must be something great about it." In other words:

WE DEVELOP A DESIRE TO GET HOOKED.

The devastating truth, which we are never told, is that all those role models drink because they, too, have been brainwashed and are addicted to alcohol.

WHY WE KEEP DRINKING

You started drinking because you were encouraged to by all the brainwashing and peer pressure. You were not drawn to it by a flaw in your genetic makeup or a weakness in your character. You were led to believe it would give you pleasure or comfort. I've said several times that there is absolutely no pleasure or comfort in drinking alcohol. The obvious next question is, if that's the case, why do we continue to drink? Why—when we have that first drink and experience how foul it tastes, or when we first get drunk and sick and hungover, or even later when we can see the harm it's causing us physically and mentally—do we keep doing it? Because we are addicted to alcohol.

You can sense that you're getting no pleasure or comfort from booze, but that doesn't mean you've seen through all the illusions. The illusion that alcohol gives you pleasure or comfort remains intact, even when you can't feel it for yourself. The nature of addiction is such that you can never get satisfaction from alcohol, but the brainwashing is so powerful that when you don't get satisfaction from drinking, you assume that you need to drink more, not less.

THE REASON YOU CONTINUE TO DRINK IS THAT YOU ARE CHASING AN IMPOSSIBLE GOAL.

The goal of satisfaction. Emotional drinkers never feel satisfied. The nature of addiction is to always leave you wanting more.

Think about the emotions that typically drive you to drink:

- Boredom—"It's something to do."

- Sadness—"It helps me forget that I'm alone."

- Stress—"It helps me switch off and forget about my worries."

- Routine—"It's just what I do at the end of the day."

- Reward—"I deserve it" when things have been tough or when celebrating success or looking for fun.

This is not a sign that drinking is a genuine pleasure. You must know what it's like to have something that gives you genuine pleasure. Let's say you enjoy swimming. People who love swimming would swim every day if they could. They wouldn't wait until they felt bored, sad, or stressed. They would shake up their routine to go swimming. And they wouldn't feel they could only swim when they'd earned it through hardship or success. They actively pursue swimming because it gives them genuine pleasure.

Next time you think about drinking for pleasure or comfort, stop and ask yourself: Am I really doing this for pleasure or comfort? Or am I doing it because something in my mind is compelling me to and making me feel uncomfortable if I don't? Pay close attention to the illusion. Can you see through it?

TWO MONSTERS

The word addict is not one that sits comfortably with anyone. You immediately think of the squalid junkie. Even smokers struggle to truly regard themselves as addicts until they understand the nature of the trap they are in. "Addict" is an ugly word that no one wants as a label, so we call ourselves smokers, drinkers, gamblers, overeaters, etc. instead. But the more we learn about addiction, the more we see that all these behaviors are addictive, and that addiction is more psychological than physical. It might be triggered by a substance, like nicotine, alcohol, or sugar, but it could just as easily be triggered by an activity, like gambling or gaming. The way it takes control of your brain is very much the same, whether it's heroin or online poker. There is a physical effect, and then there is a psychological effect.

The physical effect is so small as to be almost imperceptible, and it quickly passes, leaving a feeling of unease and emptiness, like a niggling itch. I call it the Little Monster. The Little Monster was created the first time you drank alcohol. It feeds on the drug, and when you don't give it what it wants, it begins to complain. This, too, is barely perceptible, but it is a threat because it arouses another monster.

I call this second monster the Big Monster. It lives in the brain, and it is created by all the brainwashing. When the Big Monster is aroused by the Little Monster's complaints, it interprets them as "I need a drink." So you end up trying to satisfy a craving by doing the very thing that caused the craving in the first place.

When you drink, it calms the Little Monster, creating the illusion that the alcohol has made you feel better. All it has really done is taken you from feeling miserable and restless to feeling slightly less so. Before you created the Little Monster, you may have felt miserable and restless from time to time. But the feeling wasn't permanent. You didn't need a stimulant to just feel "OK." Now you need it again and again just to feel like you're getting a little lift.

The trouble is, you never quite get back to where you were before you started. Remember how I described it in Chapter 5:

Every time you give your body a drug, you develop a tolerance against it. So every time you drink alcohol, you need to drink more to get the same effect, and every time you stop you sink lower into the trap. The longer you keep trying to satisfy the Little Monster with alcohol, the lower your mood sinks and the more dependent you feel.

Emotional drinking never makes you feel better.

MINDLESS DRINKING

Have you ever opened a bottle of wine or liquor, planning to pour yourself just one glass, only to drink the whole bottle? Why does that happen? It's not a pleasure, is it? You not only feel drunk and guilty, but emotionally you feel disgusted with yourself and frighteningly out of control. And there is absolutely no satisfaction in it.

It's further proof that no one genuinely enjoys the taste of booze. The more you drink, the less you enjoy each glass. It just becomes a process to get through the bottle until there is nothing left. Only then can you stop. You're not drinking glass after glass for any other reason than to satisfy the greedy Little Monster, and part of you can't wait to get to the point where there is no more, and you can stop.

It's the lack of satisfaction that drives you to the next glass, and the next, and the next, and the further you go without getting any feeling of satisfaction, the more impatient the drinking becomes. Like a dog chasing its tail, you go faster and faster chasing something you can never attain—perhaps eventually resorting to opening yet another bottle.

The Little Monster is the low you feel as you withdraw physically. It's made worse by the psychological craving (the Big Monster). As you slide further into the trap and become aware of the predicament you're in, it gets you down even more. You are subjected to a triple low, which becomes your new idea of normal.

The Little Monster is actually easy to put up with; it's the Big Monster that can really make you miserable. When it is stirred, it fills your head with the illusion of deprivation, bringing up all the false ideas you've been fed about alcohol being a source of pleasure and comfort, and pushing you to have another drink.

The only "pleasure" you get is the temporary respite from the Little Monster—the partial relief from the withdrawal symptoms and the mental craving. But you know that when the Little Monster starts crying again (and it always will while you keep drinking), its cries will be louder than before and the Big Monster's persuasion will be stronger than before. You end up believing that you can't enjoy anything or endure hardship without alcohol. The more you believe that to be the case, the greater the mental craving and the more dramatic the relief feels when you respond to it by drinking. No wonder you think you enjoy it. That's the Big Monster at work. This is the cycle of addiction that keeps you in the trap, even when you know you're getting no pleasure or comfort from each drink.

FACE YOUR FEAR

All emotional drinkers wish they could feel like non-drinkers, but they are afraid to "give up" their little crutch. As an emotional drinker, you know that this conflict leaves you feeling helpless and stupid. Why can't you just take control of the situation and pull yourself together?

When you're not aware of the nature of the trap you're in, the typical response to this confusion is to bury your head in the sand and pretend you don't have a problem. You have to lie to yourself about the state you're in and pretend you're in control—if it were *really* a problem, you would stop. But while your head is in the sand you won't be able to see through the illusions, and you will remain trapped, getting more and more miserable every time you drink.

The wonderful truth is that you can start feeling like a non-drinker any time you want to. All you have to do is stop drinking. It's as easy as that, as long as you understand how the trap works and follow the right method to escape.

In fact, you've already taken a big step: you've taken your head out of the sand and accepted that you have an emotional drinking problem. That's why you're reading this book. All you have to do is kill the Big Monster. Once the Big Monster is dead, you will find it easy to cut off the supply to the Little Monster, and it will die quickly and painlessly.

How do you kill the Big Monster? By removing the illusions that create the desire to drink. Remember how, and by whom, those illusions were created: the parents, friends, and other role models who brainwashed you into believing that booze is a pleasure or comfort were brainwashed themselves. The advertisers who continue to peddle that message have a vested interest in you remaining hooked.

Don't give them the satisfaction. You have a right to happiness, and they are standing in your way.

STAY RESOLUTE

You first got hooked by your brainwashed belief in the illusion of pleasure. That's what lured you into the trap. Now that you understand how the trap works, you can see that there's no genuine pleasure in drinking alcohol, only an illusion that drags you into a downward spiral of misery. You now understand that booze does not fill the void; it creates it and makes it bigger. You are unraveling the illusions.

YOU HAVE ALREADY BEGUN TO KILL THE BIG MONSTER.

It's important now that you keep your foot on the gas. There are still a number of things that could hinder your escape. There could still be a part of you that believes you get some pleasure or comfort from drinking alcohol. You might still harbor a fear that life without it will leave you feeling deprived. There are a lot of influences out there that can mislead you with false notions like these. Some of them are even well-meaning. It's crucial that you take note of my next instruction:

FIFTH INSTRUCTION: IGNORE ALL ADVICE AND INFLUENCES THAT CONFLICT WITH EASYWAY.

The fact of the matter is, you are not "giving up" anything. You are setting yourself free from a trap that has been ruining your health and happiness. Revel in this feeling! The Big Monster is already dying, and soon you will be ready to kill the Little Monster, too.

Chapter 11

SUBSTITUTES

IN THIS CHAPTER
•THE SUBSTITUTE THEORY •FLAWED LOGIC
•CUTTING DOWN •BREAK THE CHAIN

You may have been led to believe that you can solve your problem by finding an alternative that replaces alcohol in your life, but is less harmful physically and mentally. Using substitutes won't cure your addiction. In fact, it will drive you deeper into the trap.

I've talked in detail about the willpower method and why it makes quitting harder than it needs to be. It is based on the theory that if you can resist the temptation to drink long enough, your body will readjust to not having alcohol and the craving will stop. This assumes that the hardest thing about quitting is coping with the physical pangs of withdrawal.

In truth, it only takes a few days to purge your body of alcohol, but anyone who has tried to stop drinking with the willpower method knows that the craving goes on much longer than that, and even intensifies. That's because they never tackle the mental aspect that makes up 99 percent of addiction. They never kill the Big Monster.

Even so, the willpower method continues to be prescribed by doctors and other so-called experts, and to help you get through the withdrawal they recommend substitutes. With other drugs, like nicotine, they encourage addicts to take the same drug but in a "cleaner" form—for example, nicotine patches, gum, or even vaping. The thinking is that you can keep getting the drug without the harmful smoke while you focus all your efforts on breaking the "habit." Then, when you feel ready, you can gradually cut down the dose until you're able to get by without it.

But this does not recognize the way the trap works, so it serves only to keep smokers hooked on nicotine. Many so-called experts are now even suggesting that smokers continue to take nicotine in one form or another for the rest of their lives! Of course, this fails to take into account the utter misery, the control, and slavery of addiction—let alone the potential long-term physical harm caused by nicotine consumption.

So what about substitutes for alcohol? They haven't yet come up with an alternative form of administering the drug without the harmful side effects, so drinkers who try to quit with the willpower method will often replace alcohol with other drugs, most commonly nicotine or refined sugar (sugar may not be a recognized drug, but it has the same addictive effect).

When a drinker feels a craving for alcohol, they smoke a cigarette or eat candy instead. They believe it will help them withstand the cravings and give them time to break their drinking "habit," after which they can wean themselves off the cigarettes or candy as well.

FLAWED LOGIC

Can you see the fatal flaw in this approach? Actually, there are three:

1. Emotional drinking is not a habit. It's addiction.

2. The physical cravings are negligible, like a small itch. Addiction is 99 percent mental.

3. Substituting alcohol with nicotine or sugar is just swapping one addiction for another.

Like smokers, emotional drinkers believe the ritual they go through is part of the enjoyment. Opening the bottle, choosing a glass, pouring the drink, sniffing it, holding it up to the light, swirling it around, swilling it in their mouth... the way they hold the glass, the way they put it down, the way they bring it to their lips... All these rituals make drinkers think they're doing more than merely taking a drug. But the only reason they go through their ritual is to get the alcohol, and the belief that it gives them any sort of pleasure or comfort is just an illusion—the Big Monster playing tricks on them.

Think about heroin addicts. Nobody likes injections. Some of us are better than others at tolerating them, but nobody enjoys them. Heroin addicts, however, can't wait for the moment when the needle pierces their skin. Is that because they're anticipating a tremendous high? Or is it because they know it will end the terrible panic and misery they're suffering, albeit temporarily? Heroin addicts don't believe they enjoy injections. They know that the only "pleasure" they get from it is in getting their fix. There is no ritualistic pleasure in taking off tight shoes, either. You pull them off as soon as you get the chance in order to relieve the pain.

As long as you think you enjoy the ritual of drinking, you will feel deprived if you can't drink. The willpower method is designed to make you push through this feeling of deprivation, but really it intensifies it. Taking a substitute when you feel the craving for alcohol might distract you from feeling deprived, but it doesn't remove the illusion of alcohol being a pleasure or comfort. As long as that belief remains in your mind, you will remain in the trap.

Shortly after taking a substitute, the craving returns again and again. Substitutes won't help you stop craving alcohol. Substitutes only help keep the Big Monster alive.

It's actually very easy to cope with the physical pangs of withdrawal. You do it every day when you're not drinking. The Little Monster crying for its next fix is just a faint, restless feeling, like mild hunger. You don't always respond immediately, and you don't go into a panic either. You know you'll get your drink eventually, so you can ignore the faint cries easily. Most of the time you don't even notice them.

It's only when you tell yourself you can never have another drink that the Little Monster's cries induce panic. This is the Big Monster taking over, filling your mind with all those misconceptions about the pleasure and comfort you get from alcohol and triggering the fear of success. Now you can't ignore those cries; you can't concentrate on anything else until you've satisfied the craving. As long as you resist the temptation, you will feel deprived and miserable, like a child throwing a tantrum. So you placate the child with candy. Now you no longer feel deprived, but you haven't satisfied the Little Monster, so the Big Monster begins to grumble again. So you have another piece of candy, and another, and another. Before long you have an eating problem to add to your drinking problem.

CUTTING DOWN

The substitute theory is supposed to help you gradually reduce your consumption of alcohol until it's a short step to stopping altogether. As a purely physical process, this is doomed to fail. When you understand how addiction works, you know that it always makes you crave more, not less. That's because you build up a tolerance to the drug—a defense against the poison—which means you need more to feel any effect and relieve your craving. When you cut down gradually, you prevent yourself from getting the relief you crave, so your desire increases and quitting becomes even harder.

Killing the Little Monster is easy: simply stop feeding it with the drug and it will die very quickly. You don't have to give it all your focus or apply all your willpower. When you feel those faint cries, instead of interpreting them as "I need a drink," just picture the Little Monster squirming and dying inside you and enjoy the feeling for what it is—the Little Monster starving to death.

Killing the Little Monster only feels hard if you haven't already killed the Big Monster. It is the Big Monster that interprets those tiny cries as "I need a drink" and causes you to feel deprived and miserable if you think you can't have one.

Killing the Big Monster is not ending the "habit" of drinking—it's ending the desire. You end the desire as soon as you recognize that any pleasure or comfort you think alcohol gives you is merely an illusion brought on by a subtle combination of brainwashing and addiction, and that the only thing standing between you and genuine pleasure is your next drink.

If you try to quit before killing the Big Monster and removing the desire for alcohol, you will be able to make yourself abstain long enough to kill the Little Monster, but you will continue to be haunted by familiar feelings. Other triggers, like hunger or stress, will arouse the Big Monster, and the same old thought will dominate your mind: I need a drink.

For any addict who thinks they have broken the "habit" of drinking by quelling the craving with substitutes, this is devastating. You think you've overcome the physical withdrawal, but suddenly there you are craving your fix again. You start to believe that the temptation will never leave you, and you wonder how long you can resist it. With Easyway, you don't have to resist. You remove the temptation altogether.

BREAK THE CHAIN

It's the slavery of addiction that makes drinkers miserable when they find they can't quit. Trying and failing to quit makes you feel frustrated and helpless, like being chained up without any hope of escape. It's the desire to rid yourself of this feeling that is the main reason why any drinker chooses to try and quit.

There are many other reasons, of course: the poor health, the waste of money, the embarrassing behavior… but when you find yourself reaching for that bottle despite promising yourself you wouldn't, or pouring another glass even though you swore you'd just have one, it brings on a terrible mixture of negative emotions: disappointment, guilt, vulnerability, weakness, helplessness, self-loathing, frustration, despair. No wonder every emotional drinker wishes they could quit.

BY USING SUBSTITUTES, YOU SURRENDER YOURSELF TO SLAVERY FOR LIFE.

The reason you keep coming back to alcohol despite desperately wishing you didn't have to is because you feel deprived when you can't have it. You feel deprived because you believe that alcohol gives you some kind of pleasure or comfort. This illusion is perpetuated by taking substitutes.

You would only feel the need to replace alcohol with a substitute if you still had a desire for alcohol. If, when you feel the withdrawal pangs, your first thought is "I need a drink," you will always feel deprived if you don't have one, and you will want a substitute to take your mind off the craving or to reward yourself for your willpower. Either way, you are reinforcing the belief that you are depriving yourself of a pleasure or comfort by not drinking alcohol.

At the same time, you are laying yourself bare to other addictions and their accompanying risks. Substituting alcohol with cigarettes or candy might spare you the hangovers, aching liver, incontinence, and other unpleasant side effects, but it will bring its own new set of problems. Choose cigarettes and you will quickly get hooked on the world's biggest killer. Choose candy and you're buying into a substance that is responsible for global obesity and diabetes epidemics.

One day you will realize that these problems also need to be addressed. You'll stop using the substitutes and, to your dismay, you'll find that the craving for alcohol has returned. In truth, it never went away. The whole time you were taking substitutes, you were preserving the belief that alcohol gives you some kind of pleasure or comfort. The Big Monster never went away; it was just waiting for you to try and escape so it could chain you up again.

THE BIGGEST PROBLEM WITH SUBSTITUTES IS THAT THEY PERPETUATE THE ILLUSION THAT YOU'RE MAKING A SACRIFICE WHEN YOU QUIT.

We have to remove this illusion. Let's begin by looking more closely at the people who do the most to promote it: so-called "normal" drinkers.

Chapter 12

NORMAL DRINKERS

Emotional drinkers drink because they want to feel the way a non-drinker feels all the time. This is also the reason they want to quit. There is absolutely no reason, therefore, to envy any other drinker.

If you have a shingle missing from your roof and rain starts dripping in, threatening to cause untold damage, the solution is simple. Replace the shingle and the problem is solved—immediately and permanently. It might take a little time to clean up the damage from the leak, but you will find the clean-up process much easier knowing that the roof is no longer going to leak.

You can cure your drinking problem just as easily, simply by stopping the flow of alcohol. As soon as you do, you know your problem is solved and you can enjoy the process of repairing the damage. But what if you don't replace the shingle, and choose to put buckets under the leak instead? You might slow down the rate of damage to the inside of your house, but you've got the constant headache of having to empty buckets and replace them. How long are you prepared to keep doing this? Do you expect the hole in the roof to just fix itself one day?

Sooner or later, another shingle gets blown off, and the hole in the roof doubles in size. Now you're struggling to catch all the drips, and your buckets are overflowing before you can empty them. As time goes by, the flow of water gets heavier and heavier and the damage to your house is becoming disastrous. It's a nightmare, but you can make it stop any time you want, simply by fixing the roof.

If that were you, with two shingles missing, would it make sense to think, "I wish I only had one shingle missing"? Surely you'd be better off fixing the roof completely.

I'm sure you know people who seem to be able to enjoy a drink whenever they want without getting into the miserable state that you do. Problem drinkers envy these so-called "normal" drinkers and wish they could pick and choose when and how much they drank too. They haven't recognized that drinking is a source of misery that does nothing for them whatsoever; they still believe it provides some sort of pleasure or comfort and find the idea of quitting completely quite frightening. Even the lightest of drinkers balk at the prospect of never drinking—even those who go weeks between drinks. If nothing else, those people prove how weak the withdrawal pangs are that they go through them without even being aware of them. They also prove that the issue is mainly mental.

WHAT ALCOHOL REALLY DOES FOR YOU

I've been a little unfair. Alcohol isn't just a poison. For the sake of balance I should point out that it does have three genuine uses:

- An antiseptic;

- A detergent;

- A fuel.

In fact, it's similar to rubbing alcohol. Would you drink rubbing alcohol and believe it was doing you good? The one thing you don't want to do with alcohol is drink it because:

- It's a powerful poison—half a pint drunk neat will kill you.

- It's a diuretic—a drink that makes you thirsty.

- It's a highly addictive drug—80 percent or so of adults drink it and would struggles to stop doing so without help.

- It's a drain on your finances—an average drinker spends more than £50,000 on booze in a lifetime.

- It impedes judgment and concentration.

- It weakens your immune system.

- It destroys your nervous system.

- It causes stress.

- It tastes foul.

If you think it's better to be a "normal" drinker than a non-drinker, you must still believe there is some benefit to be gained from alcohol. Yet the only reason any drinker tries to limit their drinking is because they know alcohol is bad for them. They think they can control the threat by limiting the amount they drink. But they are making life very hard for themselves because:

1. They remain addicted to alcohol.

2. They spend their lives waiting for the next drink.

3. Instead of relieving the mild withdrawal pangs and mental craving whenever they feel like it, they force themselves to endure the discomfort, so they are permanently restless and feeling deprived.

4. They reinforce the illusion that drinking is enjoyable.

THE ILLUSION OF CONTROL

Problem drinkers envy "normal" drinkers because they give the impression of being in control. While you <u>know</u> that it controls you, they seem to be able to decide when they drink and how much, without any trouble at all. I repeat—"seem to." Is that really the case? Remember, all drinkers lie to give the impression that they're in control.

The fly thinks it's in control when it lands on the pitcher plant. It is confident that it can fly away at any moment. But does it? No. It continues to feed, sliding further and further into the plant, until it's too late. If you observed this, you would know that the fly is doomed from the moment it lands on the lip of the plant. If it were really in control, it would fly away while it could. But the fly is not in control. It is being controlled by the pitcher plant from the moment it picks up the scent of the nectar.

Would you say a pilot was in control if they were flying through a mountain range with inaccurate charts and the instruments had been tampered with? They might have their hands on the controls, but each decision made would be based on false information. The pilot would be unaware of the danger, so they would have no fear. But that doesn't mean the danger doesn't exist.

Can you imagine how a pilot in that situation would panic when they discovered the truth? They would not be able to relax until they'd had negotiated their way out of the mountains. But you can regain control any time you choose. All you have to do is stop taking the poison.

RASH DECISIONS

Imagine you have a pimple on your face. Someone lends you an ointment that they say will clear it up, so you rub it on and, sure enough, the pimple disappears. A week later the pimple is back, and it's bigger and redder this time. You apply more ointment and it disappears again. Five days later, the pimple returns, but now it's more than just a pimple; it's a rash. You apply more ointment but, as time goes on, the rash returns sooner and sooner, and it's bigger and itchier each time. Imagine how desperate you'd feel knowing that it's going to get worse and worse until you can find a cure. You're also so reliant on that tube of ointment that you're prepared to pay a fortune for it and you're afraid to go anywhere without it.

You're not the only one with this problem. You discover that millions of other people are in exactly the same boat, all handing over a fortune to the ointment manufacturer. So your nightmare continues, until one day you meet a friend who has neither ointment nor rash. You ask her what her secret is and she says, "Oh, I realized the ointment wasn't helping the rash. It was causing it, so I stopped using it." She tells you that if you stop applying the ointment, the rash will clear up in a few days and you'll never have to suffer from it again.

How would you feel? Would you feel miserable that you could never use the ointment again, or would you be elated that you never have to?

Can you see how this analogy applies to alcohol? Everyone who uses alcohol does so in the false belief that it's helping them in some way. The only way to stop feeling a need for alcohol is to stop using it.

THE CATAPULT

A rubber band stretches easily at first, but the resistance increases the more you stretch it. It's the same when you try to control your drinking. When you try to control the amount you drink, you have to resist the cries of the Little Monster and the "have a drink" urges of the Big Monster a little longer than usual. What effect do you think that has on your desire for alcohol? Just as the pull in the rubber band increases the more you stretch it,

THE LONGER YOU RESIST THE DESIRE FOR ALCOHOL, THE GREATER THE DESIRE BECOMES.

The more you resist the desire to drink, the more deprived you feel and the more miserable you become. It feels easy at first, when you're fired up with determination to cut down, but it gets harder and harder the longer you keep denying yourself. You keep resisting, though, because another part of your brain is feeling rather pleased with itself for taking control of the situation. You have an argument going on in your mind. One part is whining about not being able to drink, another is bragging about being in control of the rations. The result is a constant babble, dominating your mind with thoughts of your next drink.

YOU CAN'T CONTROL ALCOHOL AND BE DOMINATED BY IT AT THE SAME TIME.

Now another influence comes into play. Because you're reducing the dose of poison, and the money you waste on booze, your fear of the ill effects of drinking is lessening and your antipathy toward it is reduced. On the one hand, your desire for alcohol is increasing; on the other, you're starting to forget your reasons for wanting to cut down. The outcome is inevitable: the rubber band snaps back and catapults you deeper into the trap than you were before.

DRINKERS WHO TRY TO DRINK A CONTROLLED AMOUNT TEND TO END UP DRINKING MORE.

FALSE PRETENSES

A common ritual performed by "normal" drinkers is the discussion about who is going to drive.

"Is it my turn to drive?"

"I will if you want. I don't mind."

"Really? Are you sure it's not my turn?"

"I can't remember. I don't mind, honestly. I'll drive, you enjoy yourself."

"Well, if you insist. I think I will."

Both appear to be doing the selfless thing, but they're not being very assertive about it, are they? We all know what they're really thinking.

"Is it my turn to drive?" is cleverly designed to elicit a "no." But the partner doesn't come back with a straightforward "no;" he throws the responsibility back to her: "I will if you want." Then he adds, "I don't mind," meaning, "It's a big disappointment, but I'll stomach it."

She then expresses her relief by faking surprise at his gallantry. "Really?" Then she graciously offers him the chance to change his mind: "Are you sure it's not my turn?" Of course, for him to say, "Yes, it is your turn," would be extremely ungallant, so he feigns ignorance: "I can't remember." He's still hoping she might remember that it *is* her turn. Then he repeats the plaintive "I don't mind," hoping she'll take pity on him and feel guilty, and he really rubs it in with, "You enjoy yourself," implying that there's no chance of enjoying oneself without drinking. She reaffirms this with, "I think I will," and the first thing she does is fill her glass. She can't wait to relieve her craving.

Both partners are like prisoners drawing lots for the gallows. Neither wants to come across as so desperate to drink that they'll say, "You drive. I really have to drink tonight," but the relief of the one and the despondency of the other when it's all resolved is plain to see. "Normal" drinkers claim to get pleasure from drinking, but ask them to define that pleasure and all they offer you is defensive excuses:

"I can take it or leave it."

"I don't drink that much."

"It's not doing me any harm."

If you genuinely enjoy a drink, why would you ever choose to leave it? If drinking is a genuine pleasure, why not drink more often? The only possible reason is that you fear the effects of drinking—in which case, why do it at all?

FEAR AND PLEASURE DO NOT GO HAND IN HAND.

Many "normal" drinkers make a tradition of abstaining from alcohol for the month of January. They say it's to "detox" after the heavy drinking during the holidays. What are they trying to prove? That alcohol isn't a problem for them? What are they actually proving? That it is.

If you don't think alcohol is a problem, why go without it for a whole month? Imagine if a friend told you they were giving up bananas for January. Would you think, "There's someone who's in control of their bananas"? Or would you think, "Gosh! I didn't know she had a banana problem."

A lot of people enjoy yoga. Have you ever heard anyone explain why they go to yoga by saying, "It doesn't do me any harm"? What kind of argument is that for doing anything? The same applies to all genuine pleasures. It would be a ridiculous thing to say. When it comes to drinking, though, it's even more ridiculous to say it doesn't do you any harm, because everybody knows it does!

A PROBLEM WAITING TO HAPPEN

If you believe there is such a thing as a happy "normal" drinker, why are you not one already? All you have to do is drink less.

If I said I could fix it so that you could drink just once a week for the rest of your life, would you go for that? Better still, what if it were possible for you to control your drinking so that you did it only when you really wanted to? That's what you already do! Every time you've ever had a drink, it's been because you wanted to, even though part of your brain wished you didn't.

Do you think you'd be happier if you only drank moderately once a week? Well, do it then! What's stopping you? You've had every opportunity to be a once-a-week drinker, but you haven't taken it. Why?

The fact is, you wouldn't have been happy drinking just once a week. No drinker is. There are plenty who can stick to just one drink a week, but they're not in control. Remember the fly on the rim of the pitcher plant?

THE TENDENCY IS TO DRINK MORE, NOT LESS.

"Normal" drinkers are always fighting the urge to drink more. In normal circumstances, they manage to do so. They still believe that drinking is a source of pleasure or comfort, though, so all it takes is some kind of trauma for them to fall back on this belief and increase their drinking.

Lots of people who come to Easyway have become aware of their alcohol issue in their 30s, 40s or even later. They have spent their lives believing that drinking could give them some pleasure or comfort, but their desire to drink was never enough to outweigh their knowledge of the dangers. All it took was one trauma to tip the balance.

> ***ANYONE WHO BELIEVES IN THE ILLUSION OF PLEASURE IS IN DANGER OF DEVELOPING AN ALCOHOL PROBLEM, WHETHER THEY DRINK OR NOT.***

You should understand by now that the problem of alcoholism is not with the drinker, but with the drink. How can the same drug be beneficial for some people and devastating for others? That's as absurd as saying the rain that pours in through one missing shingle is better than the rain that pours in through two.

Alcohol provides no benefit whatsoever, other than to the industry that peddles it. There is no dividing line between "normal" drinking and problem drinking; they are both part of the same disease. The problem drinker is just at a more advanced stage.

When you started reading this book, you may have been hoping it would help you control your drinking so you could drink occasionally, like all the "normal" drinkers you know. By now you should understand that there is no place for half measures; cutting down is not an option. Every "normal" drinker is a problem drinker waiting to happen.

Chapter 13

LINGERING QUESTIONS

With every big achievement in life, there is a moment when you know you've done it—a moment of revelation. But when your big achievement is to stop doing something that's been causing you trouble, how can you feel that same sense of certainty? If you have lingering questions like this, let's address them now.

Everything I've told you so far has been aimed at correcting your mindset from the belief that alcohol gives you pleasure or comfort to the understanding that it actually creates and adds to your discomfort.

You should be thoroughly clear now that your emotional drinking issue is not due to any weakness in your character—be it a lack of willpower or an addictive personality—nor to anything special about the drug itself. If you have any lingering doubts about any of these points, remember to keep an open mind and listen to your instincts, not the Big Monster in your mind.

It's only by achieving the right mindset that you enable yourself to walk free from the trap without a painful struggle or any feeling of deprivation and sacrifice. You'll know when you've achieved that because you'll realize that the desire that keeps driving you back to drink has gone.

When you first picked up this book, you were probably keen to know how quickly it would work. How long would you have to wait before you could call yourself cured?

As you might know from experience, when you quit with the willpower method you can never be sure you've succeeded. It's a lifelong struggle to resist temptation. With Easyway, you know very clearly when you've succeeded because you remove the temptation altogether.

REPLACE UNCERTAINTY WITH KNOWLEDGE

Different people reach this stage in different frames of mind. Some are very confident that they have understood everything, and feel certain that they are ready to quit. If that's you, I'm delighted—but let's not be too hasty. You may be convinced that you never want to drink again, and that you will never try to comfort yourself with alcohol again, but beware! The trap has ways of snagging you when you least expect it. If you're not confident, please don't worry: I'm delighted for you, too. I know that all you need to do is carry on reading, follow the instructions, and you will not fail.

As I said at the start, it's essential that you complete the book, so that you can walk free with all the protection you need to make sure you never fall into the trap again.

Some people reach this stage still uncertain that they have what it takes to overcome their emotional drinking. If that's you, don't worry. We still have some ground to cover, and all will become clear. Whatever your current frame of mind, please make sure you take the time and care to read all the way to the end of the book.

It's important to make sure that you completely let go of any lingering belief in the willpower method. In Chapter 8, I explained how the reliance on willpower actually makes it harder to quit and more likely that you'll fall back into the trap. The brainwashing is so insidious that it can take a while to completely shake off the belief that overcoming the desire to drink will be difficult.

There's nothing stupid or weak about that belief. The powerful pull you feel when you try to deny your desire for alcohol may go against all your reasoning, but the feeling is still very real. So are the irritability and misery you feel when you try to use willpower to resist. You've been subjected to brainwashing your whole life, and if you have ever tried to quit with the willpower method, you have reinforced the belief that it's hard.

ANY FAILED ATTEMPT TO CONTROL YOUR DRINKING THROUGH WILLPOWER REINFORCES THE BELIEF THAT IT'S DIFFICULT TO STOP.

When you're convinced that willpower is your only weapon to overcome your drinking problem, you blame yourself for your failures. This increases your misery and low self-esteem and drives you deeper into the trap.

When you free yourself from any belief in the willpower method, all of a sudden this vicious circle goes into reverse. Stop pushing against the wrong side of the door, open your mind to the possibility that there is an easy way out and, just by believing it, that easy way will open up to you, as if by magic.

Of course, it's not magic, it's simple logic—a logic we're all blinded to by brainwashing. But when you open your mind and let the truth in, it can feel like a miracle—a moment of revelation.

Here is the simple truth:

- The desire comes from the Big Monster—the illusion that alcohol gives you pleasure or comfort.

- The anxiety you feel when you can't drink is merely the Big Monster responding to the cries of the Little Monster to be fed.

- The Little Monster was created by drinking alcohol in the first place—it's a very mild, empty, slightly insecure feeling of withdrawal.

- Therefore, drinking does not relieve the anxiety, it causes it.

Kill the Big Monster and you ensure that there's no feeling of deprivation when you stop drinking.

The willpower method is all about fighting through the anxiety in the hope that one day you will no longer feel it. In the first few days after quitting, you're full of confidence. Your willpower is at its strongest, so you have the upper hand in the battle. But over time, as you begin to think you're winning, your willpower will wane.

They say a football team is at its most vulnerable just after scoring. The same psychology applies with the willpower method. It's when you think you're winning that you're at your most susceptible. You can't keep up the huge effort it took to quit, and your motivation to do so is reduced. Then you notice the Little Monster crying to be fed, and the Big Monster wakens with a roar. It's very hard to dig in again, and you feel victory slipping from your grasp.

Now your mind is torn in two, one half determined to stay off the booze, the other urging you to stop resisting and drink. It's no surprise that we get confused, irritable, and downright miserable on the willpower method. It would be a miracle if we didn't!

If you're worried that you might fall back into the trap at some point after you've quit, because that's what you've done before, remember what it is that pulls you back in: the Big Monster. But you have all the ammunition you need to kill the Big Monster. Do that and you remove any danger of being pulled back in. Pay attention to your senses, clear your mind of the illusions, see the true picture, and you will walk free with absolute certainty that you have no desire to seek pleasure or comfort in alcohol again.

WILL I BE ABLE TO HAVE FUN?

This is a crucial question. This book is all about helping you put the pleasure back into your life by taking alcohol out of it. The problem has been that you've been trying to obtain pleasure in life by drinking alcohol. You should now be clear that alcohol is NOT the solution to emotional issues or a quest for pleasure.

But it's understandable that if you've spent years of your life believing that booze gives you pleasure or comfort, you might worry that living the rest of your life without it will be joyless. That's why it's so important to unravel the brainwashing. The truth is that addiction to alcohol actually reduces your ability to take pleasure or comfort from anything.

If you believe you can't be happy without booze, you won't be. With the willpower method, you never really remove this belief.

WHEN YOU NO LONGER HAVE THE DESIRE FOR ALCOHOL, YOU DON'T SEE IT AS A TREAT. YOU DON'T MISS IT BECAUSE IT MAKES NO CONTRIBUTION TO YOUR ENJOYMENT. IN FACT, IT NEVER DID.

The brainwashing creates a romanticized idea of alcohol in the drinker's mind. In many cases, the things they think they'll miss are situations they haven't even experienced for real. They're just fantasies. When they have experienced enjoyable situations involving alcohol, it quickly becomes apparent that there were other aspects that made it enjoyable, such as the presence of friends, an exciting location, a celebratory mood, etc.

If you have memories of occasions like this that you consider to have been enjoyable because you were drinking, go over them carefully to understand why the booze appeared to enhance the situation, and see that in reality it was more likely to do the opposite. Instead of worrying that such occasions won't be enjoyable again without drinking, see through the illusion and flip it on its head. Remind yourself that you'll now be able to enjoy those occasions MORE because you'll be FREE from the slavery of emotional drinking. All your senses will be heightened when you are free—everything feels even better. And I do mean everything!

On most occasions, you're not even aware of how you feel while you're drinking. The only time you're really aware of how alcohol makes you feel is when you want it but can't have it, or when you're drinking it but wish you weren't. In both cases the feeling is the same: miserable. The conclusion is obvious:

TAKE AWAY THE BOOZE AND
YOU REMOVE THE MISERY.

WILL I BE ABLE TO COPE IN HARD TIMES?

Another crucial question—possibly even more so. Emotional drinking is mostly triggered by negative emotions and the need for comfort. A family argument, pressure at work, financial worries, a trauma... You can take yourself out of the situation for a while, focus on drinking, and put your problems out of your mind.

The trouble is, the problems don't go away, do they? Sooner or later you have to return to the real world—and the problems are still there waiting for you. In fact, they've usually become worse. If you believe that alcohol can provide comfort in these situations, you're going to be vulnerable after you've quit. The next time you need to be comforted, the Big Monster will pull you back into the trap.

Think about it logically: how is drinking going to help you solve any of the problems in your life? Have you ever told yourself, in the middle of an argument, "It doesn't matter that we're shouting horrible, hurtful things at each other, because I can just pour myself a drink and everything will be all right"?

Or, come to think of it, didn't the fact that you're hooked on booze make you feel worse?

Stressful situations are part of life. Everyone goes through them, but not everyone gets in a huff because they can't drink. Accept that you'll have ups and downs after you've quit, and understand that if you start yearning for a drink in such situations, you'll be pining for an illusion and opening up a void.

EMOTIONAL DRINKING REDUCES YOUR ABILITY TO COPE WITH STRESSFUL SITUATIONS BY ADDING TO THE STRESS.

You can be completely clear about this right now, while you're fired up and ready to quit, but still quickly feel confused and vulnerable when hard times occur and you find yourself feeling low again. It can make you think you're falling back into the trap.

In order to avoid this potential pitfall, anticipate the difficult times that will inevitably occur after you've quit, and prepare yourself for them mentally.

- Remind yourself that any stress you feel is not because you can't drink.

- Tell yourself, "OK, this is tough, but at least I don't have the added problem of being a slave to alcohol. I am stronger now."

Without emotional drinking, you WILL be stronger and, because of that, you'll find that stressful situations will actually feel less severe.

BEING FREE ENHANCES ALL SITUATIONS IN LIFE—GOOD AND BAD—THE HIGHS FEEL HIGHER AND THE LOWS NOT NEARLY AS LOW.

THE MOMENT OF REVELATION

Soon you will be ready to go through a ritual: "the final drink." Afterwards, you'll be able to say that you are no longer addicted to alcohol, you have no desire for it, and you are free from emotional drinking. If you've already abstained from alcohol, you do not need to have a final drink... just go through the rest of the ritual, confirming that you've already had your final drink. This ritual has a very specific purpose: to draw a line in the sand. It marks the point at which you walked free from the trap. It is not necessarily the moment when you realize you are free. It's important to understand that you become a non-drinker the moment you've decided that you've had your last drink. To become a drinker again, you'd have to start drinking again.

The final drink is the act of walking out of the prison. When you've been stuck in prison for a long time and then the door suddenly swings open, you may sit and savor the moment for a while before walking out. In other words, the moment of freedom and the moment of escape may come at different times. When you achieve something big in life, you experience a wonderful, developing high as the realization of your achievement sinks in. A lot of people feel this when they quit with Easyway—a moment of revelation. The confusion they felt as an addict is suddenly replaced by absolute clarity and understanding—a thrilling realization that their desire for alcohol has gone.

It's essential to achieve this clarity. It is not enough to *try* or *hope* that you will never get hooked again—those are the traits of the willpower method. You have to be certain. Easyway is designed to give you that certainty. Unlike the willpower method, Easyway doesn't keep you waiting for some sign of confirmation that you are cured. You won't spend the rest of your life suspecting that there could be bad news waiting just around the corner.

YOU KNOW YOU'RE FREE AS SOON AS YOU DECIDE YOU HAVE HAD YOUR FINAL DRINK.

Chapter 14

YOU ARE NOT ALONE

IN THIS CHAPTER

•*SECRET DRINKERS* •*MEN AND WOMEN*
•*PICKERS AND CHOOSERS* •*DRINKING LESS IS NOT THE CURE*

We've established that there is no such thing as a "normal" drinker. All drinkers are in the same trap as you, and they all feel alone with the problem, regardless of how they might appear on the outside. It's important that you see that you are not alone with your emotional drinking issue and that, however you go about fueling your addiction, the instructions for quitting apply to you in exactly the same way as they do for everybody else.

For every uncomfortable emotion there is a type of emotional drinking. You may regard yourself as different from other emotional drinkers because your problem seems so particular to you, and this might lead you to suspect that Easyway may not be able to set you free. Let me state this very clearly:

ALL EMOTIONAL DRINKERS HAVE
THE SAME PROBLEM.

IN FACT ALL DRINKERS ARE EMOTIONAL DRINKERS!

Easyway is a proven method of tackling that problem. If you choose to believe that you are beyond the help of Easyway, you will only guarantee that you remain in the trap. The only reason you might choose to remain in the trap is the fear of what life will be like if you succeed. If you haven't yet overcome the fear of success, go back and read the last chapter again. It's essential that you remove any doubts about your decision to quit, and recognize that you will not be losing anything, only making wonderful gains.

SECRET DRINKERS

We all know about secret drinkers. They spend their lives living a lie. They lie to themselves that they get pleasure or comfort from alcohol, and they lie to other people that they don't drink at all! They're so ashamed of their drinking that they go to great lengths to hide it.

This constant pressure to cover their tracks is highly stressful and can lead to higher and higher risks and, of course, a greater desire to drink. It also takes a heavy toll on their self-respect, which only compounds feelings of loneliness and anxiety.

There's a bit of the secret drinker in all emotional drinkers. Drinking alcohol requires you to lie to yourself, because there is no logic to it. You know it makes no sense. You wish you could stop, and you don't understand why you can't. If you were completely honest about your problem, you would admit that there is no pleasure or comfort in it, but you can't do that because it's the only reason you have for continuing to do it.

Believe me, one of the greatest pleasures of escaping from the trap is never having to lie to yourself again. The release, the sense of freedom, is amazing.

MEN AND WOMEN

Emotional drinking afflicts men just as it does women, despite the general perception that it's more of a problem for women. Men are exposed to the same brainwashing from birth, and men turn to drinking to tackle difficult emotions too.

The physical effects are no more fun for a man than they are for a woman: losing control, going on a bender, wishing you could stop, but feeling powerless to change—all are as miserable and unnerving for men as they are for women.

The point is that your emotional drinking problem has nothing to do with your gender. The illusions that keep you in the trap are the same for everybody, and the temptation for both sexes is growing all the time.

As you unravel the brainwashing, it's also worth noticing how the alcohol industry targets specific groups. It is one of the most sophisticated and ruthless marketing machines of all. Some products are aimed at women, and some are aimed at men. Be aware that you are being targeted, and if you find yourself hooked on a particular type of drink, that's not because the drink is tailormade for you; it's because someone has made the decision to hook you.

You don't get hooked because you're weak or prone to addiction or ill-disciplined or any of these false beliefs. It's not a flaw in your character or DNA. You get hooked because there's a Big Monster in your brain that feeds you false messages every time you feel the slightest emotional prompt.

PICKERS AND CHOOSERS

I wrote in the last chapter about so-called "normal" drinkers and their apparent ability to drink whenever and whatever they want. Remember that such people don't actually exist. No one who drinks is in any more control than you are. You relinquish control the moment you land on the edge of the pitcher plant and only regain it when you stop drinking. Don't let the apparent ease with which other people drink make you feel different and alone. You might think it sounds like a nice prospect to only feel the urge to drink every now and then. But wouldn't it be nicer to never want to do it at all? Imagine how free you would feel!

The reason you drink more than you think is ideal is because you make yourself. When you believe that alcohol gives you pleasure or comfort, the natural urge is to drink more. But drinking more makes you miserable too. That's the fiendish ingenuity of the trap; as long as you're in, it doesn't matter whether you do it more or less often. You become increasingly miserable either way.

DRINKING LESS IS NOT THE CURE

Remember what we said about cutting down in Chapter 11. Addiction makes you want to take more of the drug, not less, so by trying to cut down on the amount you drink, you are forcing yourself to suffer more and longer mental cravings. Trying to fill these periods with substitutes doesn't work, because it doesn't tackle the brainwashing. In other words, you keep believing that alcohol gives you some sort of pleasure or crutch, so you feel deprived while you're making yourself do without.

So-called Pickers and Choosers, who seem able to take or leave alcohol, are doing this to themselves all the time. Cutting down reduces their chances of quitting because:

1. It increases the value they place on their little fix.

2. It weakens their resolve to quit.

With Easyway, there is no cutting down and there is no need for substitutes. There is one very simple reason for this:

CUTTING DOWN AND USING
SUBSTITUTES DOESN'T WORK.

In fact, trying to cut down is unsustainable and usually results in you drinking more than before.

Substitutes are also counterproductive for two big reasons:

1. They perpetuate the myth that withdrawal is an ordeal.

2. They keep the Big Monster alive.

We'll look more closely at withdrawal in the next chapter. The key thing to remember is that it's not your body that needs help to break free—it's your mind. The only way to free your mind from the tyranny of addiction is to kill the Big Monster.

As you'll soon discover, this is a wonderful moment. You'll know immediately that you're free, and the idea of cutting down will be ridiculous. Why crawl out of the prison when you can take one glorious step?

Chapter 15

WITHDRAWAL

IN THIS CHAPTER
•*A MILD, EVERYDAY FEELING* •*NO CAUSE FOR PANIC*
•*THE PLEASURE OF WITHDRAWAL*
•*WHEN WILL I BEGIN TO RELAX?*

The so-called pain of withdrawal is one of the myths that hold addicts back from trying to quit, the fear of the withdrawal period is founded on false assumptions. Withdrawal symptoms are nothing out of the ordinary, and when you quit with Easyway, they become a source of pleasure, not pain.

Addicts talk about withdrawal as if it is something that only happens when you try to quit. In fact, addicts experience withdrawal symptoms every day and think nothing of them. As I have explained, withdrawal is part of the repetitive addiction cycle: you take the drug, you withdraw. Every time you take the drug it triggers the next set of withdrawal pangs as it leaves your body. Addicts describe this as an empty, slightly restless feeling—nothing more severe than that.

The feeling triggers the desire for the next drink. Physically, it's so slight you can hardly feel it. This is the Little Monster. If your mind happens to be occupied with something else, you can easily get by without noticing the feeling at all. It's when the Little Monster awakens the Big Monster in your brain that the craving is triggered and starts to nag.

Most emotional drinkers respond to this by having a drink, so they never really become conscious of the withdrawal symptoms. They are slight. So when you fear that quitting will be hard because you'll have to go through the pain of withdrawal, what you're actually fearing is a tiny sensation that you already feel several times a day—and that amounts to nothing more than a slightly empty feeling.

If the physical effects of withdrawal were as bad as they're supposed to be, do you think you could go for hours without having a drink? But that's what millions of drinkers manage to do every night when they're asleep, and when they wake up, they're not in agony.

The physical effects of withdrawal are only a problem when they arouse the Big Monster. If you've killed the Big Monster, the cravings disappear and all you're left to contend with is the mild withdrawal.

NO CAUSE FOR PANIC

Most addicts are familiar with the panic that sets in when you feel the withdrawal pangs but you don't know where your next fix is coming from. Having said that, it's a panic that many addicts have never actually experienced—but they can imagine it. A common trait of all addicts is to go to great lengths to ensure they never have to go through that panic. Smokers, for example, will keep a spare pack of cigarettes with them at all times; drinkers will make sure they have a stash of booze somewhere in the house. It's their security against panic.

The obvious downside to stockpiling is that you descend into the trap faster because you always have your fix available— you never have to wait. This helps answer the question about why some people become more hooked than others. The fear of withdrawal and the cravings speeds up the cycle of addiction.

Withdrawal is not painful, but if you expect it to be then it will become a problem. It creates mental cravings in response to withdrawal. The fear of pain causes the panic. There is no actual pain, contrary to what you may have read elsewhere. You've probably read that quitting brings on withdrawal symptoms such as:

- Tiredness;

- Headaches;

- An upset stomach;

- Weak and aching muscles;

- Heart palpitations;

- The shakes;

- The sweats;

- The shivers;

- Breathing difficulties.

It's no coincidence that these are all symptoms of chronic anxiety. They are not caused by withdrawal from alcohol; they are caused by the mental panic brought on by the fear of withdrawal. In other words:

THE FEAR OF WITHDRAWAL
DISCOMFORT IS SELF-FULFILLING.

People who quit with Easyway don't experience these symptoms. Even if you did, is that really something to fear? These so-called withdrawal symptoms are very similar to the symptoms of influenza. Nobody wants to get the flu, but does the thought of it make you panic? No doubt you've had the flu before and probably expect to get it again. Does that thought make you panic? You know you can get through it in a few days. Would you not exchange a few days of the flu for freedom from your emotional drinking issue?

When you know the cause of pain or discomfort, it becomes much easier to endure. You can try it for yourself. Dig your fingernails into your leg and gradually increase the pressure. You'll find you can endure quite a severe level of pain without any sense of fear or panic. That's because you're in control. You know what's causing the pain, and you know that you can make it stop whenever you choose. But if you started feeling a pain like that in your leg and didn't know what was causing it or how bad it was going to get, you would start to panic.

People who quit with the willpower method expect to go through a physical ordeal, but they don't know how bad it's going to be. They've heard it can be bad, so they're anxious. This anxiety increases the ordeal. In fact, the physical sensation is very slight— so slight that you feel it every day and don't even notice it. But if you feel that sensation and don't understand why, or how bad it's going to get, and you can't do anything about it, that's when the panic sets in and the symptoms of anxiety follow.

You can see this in any addict when they are denied their fix. They become restless and fidgety. They develop nervous tics and are constantly doing things with their hands or grinding their teeth. These are the physical signs of the empty, insecure feeling triggering mental cravings, and if it is allowed to develop it can quickly turn into frustration, irritability, anxiety, anger, fear, and panic. Non-drinkers don't suffer from this restlessness or the cravings. Get it clear in your mind that drinking alcohol causes this feeling; it doesn't relieve it. As long as you understand that, you don't need to feel any sense of panic when you quit.

With Easyway, the withdrawal period is easy to get through because you know exactly what causes the empty, restless feeling and you know that it will pass soon. You are in control. You also know that the one thing that will ensure that you suffer from that feeling for the rest of your life is to keep drinking. So when you feel the slight physical symptoms of withdrawal, they won't make you panic; they'll trigger a wonderful sense of freedom.

THE PLEASURE OF WITHDRAWAL

After you've had your Final Drink and your new life as a non-drinker has begun, you'll still continue to feel the withdrawal for a few days. Just remind yourself that this is not physical pain; it's only the faint cries of the Little Monster wanting to be fed. You could easily ignore it, but there's no need to do that.

This is a good time to reinforce your knowledge that the Little Monster was created when you first started drinking, and it has continued to feed on every subsequent drink you've had. Now that you have stopped drinking, you have cut off the supply and that horrible Little Monster is dying. Feel no mercy!

As it dies, the Little Monster will writhe around and beg you to feed it. Create a mental image of this monster getting weaker and weaker, and enjoy starving it to death. Keep this mental image with you at all times to help make sure you don't respond to its pleadings by lapsing into thinking, "I need a drink." Drinking would only prolong the withdrawal feeling.

Be ruthless. Take delight in feeling the Little Monster die. Before, when you've tried to quit with the willpower method, the feeling made you miserable because it was a reminder that you couldn't have a drink. Now it's a cause for celebration because it's a reminder that you don't have to! Even if, for a few days, you do find yourself thinking "I need a drink," don't think you've failed.

It's nothing to worry about. Thoughts don't count—it's how you react to thoughts that matters. If you believe the thought, you'll be miserable—you'll crave a drink—but if you understand that the thought has occurred because you momentarily forgot that you've stopped, you can pause for a moment, feel calm, and remind yourself how lucky you are to be free. In fact, the more you think it, the happier you'll be.

WHEN WILL I BEGIN TO RELAX?

You can enjoy the withdrawal period, knowing it's a sign that the Little Monster is dying—but how long until it passes altogether and you can go back to enjoying life?

With Easyway, you can start enjoying the many genuine pleasures of being a non-drinker from the minute you kill the Big Monster. This is not like the willpower method, where you keep waiting for something to *not* happen. The withdrawal period will not occupy your mind to such an extent that you can't focus on anything else. It's just that when it does occupy your mind, you're ready for it, rather than it causing you distress or concern—it creates moments of real joy.

The normal amount of time for the Little Monster to die is a few days. That's all. A few days for the slight physical pangs to pass. You can put it right out of your mind to such an extent that, after about three weeks, there comes a moment when you suddenly realize that you haven't thought about drinking for quite a while. It's an amazing feeling, but for those who quit with the willpower method it can be a dangerous moment. You feel great. You feel powerful. You feel in control. It's time to celebrate. What possible harm could it do to reward yourself with a little drink?

The Big Monster is not dead, and sooner or later it will drag you back into the trap.

With Easyway, you won't feel like celebrating with a drink. That's because you won't feel that you've made a sacrifice or that drinking is any kind of reward. The desire for alcohol has gone completely because you understand that it does nothing for you. All drinking will do for you now is drag you back into the trap.

So you can relax from the moment you complete your final drink, or confirm that you've already had your final drink, and realize that the desire has gone. When you feel the withdrawal pangs, instead of responding with, "I need a drink," you can remind yourself, "I don't ever have to go through that misery again—I'm free!"

FALSE COMFORT

Fear is the big obstacle that prevents addicts from quitting. How you allay that fear is important. Some addicts try to do so by telling themselves they can always start again if it gets too hard. In other words, they'll try, but they give themselves a get-out clause. This might give them the courage to try to quit, but it won't enable them to succeed.

If you see falling back into the trap as some kind of safety net, then you still regard alcohol as a form of pleasure or comfort and you have not killed the Big Monster. Instead of giving yourself a get-out clause, start off with the certainty in your mind that you're going to be free forever. To achieve that certainty, you have to remove the fear and panic.

Chapter 16

TAKING CONTROL

One of the most upsetting aspects of emotional drinking is the feeling of being out of control. The aim of Easyway is not just to help you quit drinking, but also to help you rediscover the feeling of control over your life and your actions. It begins when you kill the Big Monster.

Ask an emotional drinker why they want to quit and you'll get a variety of answers. There's the physical damage of being a drinker: getting drunk and sick; losing your judgment; hurting yourself. There's the social impact: having to lie to people; making a fool of yourself; saying things you later regret. And then there's the psychological impact: the loss of self-respect; the frustration and disappointment; the fear.

Despite being bombarded by misinformation about the so-called benefits of alcohol, all emotional drinkers are aware of the dangers, and any one of these factors, or a combination of several, could be the motivation that drives you to quit. It's only when you succeed in becoming a non-drinker that you appreciate the biggest gain of all:

ESCAPE FROM SLAVERY.

When you're in the alcohol trap, the temptation to drink is so great, you find any excuse to keep doing it. The logic of quitting gets pushed aside.

"It's not doing me any harm."

"I can handle it."

"I can quit any time I want."

These flimsy excuses for drinking are not positive arguments at all; they are defensive cover-ups for the fact that you don't have any of the control you claim to. It IS doing you harm. You CANNOT handle it. And you've proven time and time again that you CAN'T QUIT any time you want.

As an emotional drinker, you know and hate the fact that you're not in control, but you refuse to confront the slavery. No one likes to think of themselves as a slave. As humans, we pride ourselves on being in control. The heaviest addicts tend to be very strong-willed people who have enjoyed a high degree of control over most of their lives, and it infuriates them to think they're being controlled by something. It's in our nature to believe that we should be able to conquer our addictions through sheer force of will. And it leaves us depressed and irritable when we find we can't.

The key that enables addicts to break free is the realization that they can end their days of slavery not through struggle, but simply by walking away. The facts are very straightforward:

- You no longer need to be a slave to a drug that does absolutely nothing for you.

- You will not miss it.

- You will enjoy life more.

- You will be better able to deal with stress.

- You won't have to go through some terrible trauma in order to escape.

MAKE A CHOICE

Nobody is forcing you to drink. Every drinker chooses to drink. Every time you open a bottle, pour a glass, or get your fix, you're exercising your personal choice. That might seem contradictory to what I just said about slavery. How can a slave exercise personal choice?

It is the twisted nature of addiction and the trap you're in. As an emotional drinker, you're not in control, but you're the one making the decision to drink. You're controlled to believe that you're making choices that are good for you. You weigh what you know about the risks against your beliefs about the hardships of quitting, and you make a choice that it's better to stay in the trap.

It's a choice you hate yourself for making, but the alternative is worse—or so you've been led to believe.

In every addict's mind, this struggle between logic and illusion is constant. It's confusing and frustrating. It makes you feel foolish and weak. That's not a pleasant feeling, so you go into denial and pretend it's not happening in order to avoid the painful truth about what you've become: a hopeless, pathetic slave to alcohol. Instead of facing up to this grim reality and making the one move that will free you—quitting drinking—you search for excuses to keep doing it.

It's only when you face up to the extent of your problem and accept that you've become a slave to a diabolical monster that you can escape from the trap. So if you want to regain control, it's essential that you recognize and understand that alcohol controls you, not the other way around, and that it is not the solution to your misery, but the cause.

In the previous chapter, I talked about withdrawal pangs and how they should become a source of joy. This is part of the process of taking control. When the cries of the Little Monster don't make you think, "I need a drink," and instead make you think, "Great, the Little Monster is suffering and will soon die." That's when you know you're winning.

You took your first positive step in taking control of your emotional drinking issue when you chose to read this book. You could have chosen to bury your head in the sand and carry on stumbling further and further into the trap, but you chose to take positive action to cure yourself. That might seem like a long way back now, but you showed that you still have the power to make a positive choice. Now all you have to do is keep making positive choices and you will soon experience the moment of revelation.

THREE KEY FACTS

While you are getting very close to the moment when you perform the ritual of the Final Drink and make a solemn vow never to drink again, there are three very important facts that I want you to remember:

1. ALCOHOL DOES ABSOLUTELY NOTHING FOR YOU AT ALL.

It is essential that you understand why this is the case and accept it, so that you never feel deprived.

2. THERE IS NO NEED FOR A GRADUAL TRANSITION.

Despite what you may have heard elsewhere, it is not necessary to go through a withdrawal period when curing an addiction. It may take time to repair the damage caused by your drinking, but the moment you stop believing that you need alcohol for pleasure or comfort is the moment you become free. You don't have to wait for anything *not* to happen.

3. THERE IS NO SUCH THING AS "JUST THIS ONCE" OR "THE OCCASIONAL BINGE."

If you're still tempted by booze, the Big Monster is still alive and will pull you back into the trap. You have to remove any desire to drink, and that means understanding and believing the fact that it does absolutely nothing for you whatsoever. If the thought of drinking enters your head, that's not a problem as long as you react by using the thought to remind yourself that you're free.

KILLING THE BIG MONSTER

The Big Monster is the enemy of all addicts. It is the persuasive influence that cons you into believing that you get some sort of pleasure or comfort from alcohol, and it is the fiendish tyrant that makes you fear your life will be incomplete without it. The Big Monster convinces you that booze is your friend, your support, and even your identity. It makes you feel that quitting will be like losing your closest companion, or even a part of yourself.

When you lose a friend, it grieves you. Over time the grieving eases, and you continue with your life, but you're always left with a genuine void that you can never fill. There's nothing you can do about it. It's a fact of life. You have no choice but to accept the situation and, although it still hurts, you do.

Addicts who try to quit by using willpower also feel a void and a sense of loss. Even though they know they're making the right decision to stop, they believe it comes at a price—the sacrifice of their little crutch. They have not been told about the Big Monster and they believe that all those ideas about the benefits of alcohol are true. So they mope and grieve, as if mourning for a friend—but this false friend isn't even dead. The temptation to resurrect it stays with them for the rest of their life.

When you know and understand about the Big Monster, you can easily see that it is your mortal enemy, the sole cause of your drinking misery, so there is no moping or grieving when you rid yourself of it—only joy and celebration from the start. And every time that Big Monster crosses your mind, you can continue to rejoice and celebrate for the rest of your life.

So your mindset is crucial as you set about destroying the Big Monster. You have to be absolutely clear that alcohol is not your friend, not your support, not your identity. It never has been. In fact, it's an evil monster hell-bent on destroying you by twisting your perception and forcing you to make harmful choices. By killing it, you're sacrificing nothing; you're just making wonderful, positive gains.

The beauty of killing the Big Monster is that you don't need my words to convince you of these gains; you will instantly feel them for yourself. So if you're wondering, "When will I kill the Big Monster?" the answer is, quite simply, whenever you choose to. You could spend the next few days, and possibly the rest of your life, continuing to believe that alcohol is your friend and wondering when you'll stop missing it. Do that and you'll feel miserable; the desire for alcohol may never leave you, and you'll either end up feeling deprived for the rest of your life, or you'll end up falling back into the trap and feeling even worse.

Or you can recognize alcohol for the mortal enemy it really is and take pleasure in cutting it out of your life. Do that and you'll never have to crave it again. Whenever it enters your mind, you'll feel elated that it is no longer ruining your life.

Make no mistake, it will enter your mind. For people who quit with the willpower method, that's a problem—a constant reminder of something they think they're missing. But for you, it won't be a problem. It'll be a joy—a constant reminder of something you've overcome. So unlike people who quit with the willpower method, you'll have no need to try and block it from your mind. In fact, it's important that you don't. Trying not to think about something is a sure way of becoming obsessed with it. For example, if I tell you not to think about elephants, what's the first thing that comes into your head?

Exactly!

When you can think about alcohol with nothing but joy that you've banished it from your life, that's when you know you've regained control.

BUILD YOUR DEFENSES

As well as preparing your mindset to destroy the Big Monster, you need to prepare for the period after you've had your final drink. During the first few days in particular, you might actually forget that you've quit. That may sound surprising, but it can happen at any time. You catch yourself thinking, "I'll have a drink." Then you remember you don't do that anymore. But you wonder why the thought entered your head.

It's really nothing more sinister than when you buy a new car and the controls are in different places. For the first few days, every time you try to use your turn signal, you squirt water over the windshield. You didn't want to do that; you wanted to use the turn signal. You just forgot you were in your new car. It doesn't bother you; you know that before long you'll adjust.

It's crucial in these circumstances that you don't allow doubt to creep into your mind. It's perfectly normal for certain everyday cues to trigger your old responses to alcohol. When alcohol has been such a dominant part of your life, of course it's going to take a while for you to shake off your old routines. Natural cravings like hunger can be a trigger too. If you allow these moments to rattle your resolve and make you question whether you really have killed the Big Monster, it can be disastrous. You need to prepare for these situations so you're not caught off guard, you remain calm and, instead of thinking, "I can't have a drink," you think, "Isn't it great?! I don't need to drink any more. I'm free!"

Forgetting for a moment that you no longer drink isn't a bad sign; it's a very good one. It's proof that your life is returning to the happy state you were in before you got hooked, when emotional drinking didn't dominate your whole existence.

So expect these moments to happen and be prepared for them. Then you won't get caught off guard. Build yourself a suit of impregnable armor now, while you're preparing for your final drink. You know you're making the right decision and nothing will be able to make you doubt it. That way these moments, instead of being the cause of your downfall, can be a source of strength, security, and immense pleasure, reminding you just how wonderful it is to be... **_FREE!_**

SHOUT IT FROM THE ROOFTOPS

Having the confidence to be real and honest about your emotional drinking problem is the surest sign that you're regaining control. You were honest with yourself when you made the decision to read this book. Now I strongly encourage you to share your story with anyone you've been hiding it from.

If you're worried that people will lose respect for you, you'll be surprised. It's far more likely that they will respect you for your honesty and strength in doing something about your addiction, and they will support you all the way. Keeping your addiction covered up (or thinking you are) is incredibly stressful and damaging to your self-respect.

Chances are, the people you think you've been hiding your addiction from haven't been deceived at all. They've probably noticed the change in your behavior. They may have felt the sting of your irritability. They might have become suspicious of your inability to apply yourself to work and other commitments. The longer you go on trying to deceive people, the more their feelings will grow into distrust and dislike. Tell the truth and you give them the opportunity to understand why your behavior has been so erratic and help you deal with it. Don't be surprised if they're relieved by the news.

More importantly, you will take a huge weight off your shoulders. Deceit is part of the slavery of addiction. You'll be amazed how good it feels to be free from it. You can look forward to:

- More time for work and play;

- A greater ability to concentrate;

- A greater ability to cope with stress;

- The rediscovery of genuine pleasures;

- Better health;

- A sharper, brighter, happier state of mind;

- Real control over your life.

All that said, please don't feel worried, if you would rather keep your new-found freedom to yourself. You are about to impress the most important person on the planet: you! That's all that really counts.

The moment has come for you to take control and escape from the emotional drinking trap. Congratulations! You deserve to feel very excited. Enjoy the process of escape. Look forward to all the benefits you are about to enjoy. And whenever the thought of alcohol enters your mind, don't feel miserable because you can't drink. Think, "YES! I don't have to do that anymore. I'm FREE!"

Chapter 17

THE FINAL DRINK

IN THIS CHAPTER
• *THE REAL OBJECTIVE* • *YOUR MENTAL CHECKLIST*
• *CHOOSE YOUR MOMENT* • *YOUR FINAL DRINK*
• *AND THAT'S IT! YOU'RE FREE!*

The time has come to complete your escape. I've armed you with all the information you need to break free and start enjoying life as a happy non-drinker. The moment has arrived for you to mark the occasion. Are you ready? Here's to success!

A major problem with the willpower method is that it leaves the drinker unclear about what they're trying to achieve. On the surface, it's really quite straightforward: you want to quit drinking. If you've understood everything I've said about so-called "normal drinkers" and "cutting down," you'll be quite clear that quitting means quitting for life. It doesn't mean you can have the occasional drink.

But if you define success as not drinking for the rest of your life, how will you know if you've succeeded? This is the problem that people who quit with the willpower method face. They can only ever know if they've succeeded when they're on their deathbed. Who wants to wait that long?

If your definition of success is never drinking again, you'll spend the rest of your life waiting to see if you fail. Do you really want that uncertainty hanging over you for the rest of your life?

The objective, then, is not to HOPE you'll never drink again, but to KNOW you'll never drink again. Easyway gives you that certainty, and the ritual of the final drink marks your success. It is the line in the sand that you cross with absolute certainty that you will never drink again. As I mentioned already, if you have abstained for a long period you should not have a final drink— instead, just confirm to yourself that you have already done so.

I've said that people who quit with the willpower method can never be sure they won't drink again. They can only hope and try. So how is Easyway different?

Let's say I asked you if you thought you'd ever take arsenic. Of course you would say no. Why? Because you know that arsenic is a lethal poison, and nobody in their right mind would poison themselves. But what if you were immune to arsenic, so it couldn't do you any harm. Would you take it?

I can predict with reasonable confidence that the answer is still no, and your reason would be something like, "Why would I want to take it?"

It's not the absence of disadvantages that make you want to take something, it's the advantages. And when there are no advantages, you have absolutely no reason to take it, so you can say with absolute certainty that you won't.

You know that there are no advantages to drinking alcohol. It does nothing for you whatsoever. You have seen through the illusions that made you think it gave you some kind of pleasure or comfort. So you have no reason to ever want to drink again.

That level of certainty is what you are aiming for: not just giving up alcohol, but putting your final drink behind you with the absolute certainty that you will never drink again.

YOUR MENTAL CHECKLIST

If you're not feeling that certainty, if you have doubts about what you are about to do, don't panic. Remember the importance of following all the instructions in order. With each instruction I've given you, you should have been able to follow it without any problem. If not, go back and re-read that section.

The code word RATIONALIZED will help you identify any gaps in your understanding. This serves as both a reminder and a checklist. Go through each item and ask yourself:

- Do I understand it?

- Do I agree with it?

- Am I following it?

R   REJOICE!

You're freeing yourself from a tyrant. (See Chapter 3)

A   ADVICE

Ignore it if it conflicts with Easyway. (See Chapter 10)

T   TIMING

Do it now! (See this chapter)

I   IMMEDIATE

You don't have to wait for anything *not* to happen. (See Chapter 16)

O   ONE BINGE

Is all it takes to hook you again. (See Chapter 14)

N   NEVER

Seek pleasure or comfort from alcohol. (See Chapter 12)

A   ADDICTIVE PERSONALITY

There's no such thing. (See Chapter 9)

L   LIFESTYLE

Rediscover genuine pleasures. (See Chapter 16)

I   INCREMENTAL CURES

Cutting down and using substitutes keep you trapped. (See Chapters 14 and 15)

Z   ZERO SACRIFICE

You are not "giving up" <u>anything</u>. (See Chapter 7)

E   ELEPHANTS

Don't try not to think about drinking. (See Chapter 16)

D   DOUBT

Never doubt your decision to quit. (See Chapter 7)

If you're clear on all the points in the RATIONALIZED checklist and you've followed and understood all the instructions, then you should be feeling certain that you have destroyed the Big Monster. You may have felt a rush of relief and clarity, a moment of revelation. If you haven't, don't worry. The realization dawns on different people in different ways. What matters is that the Big Monster is dead. As long as you're confident of that, you're ready for the ritual of the final drink. So when would be the ideal time to do it?

CHOOSE YOUR MOMENT

This is a common dilemma for addicts. Because it's such an important step in your life, the tendency is to choose a standout occasion, like a birthday or New Year's Eve. I advise you not to. These "special" days have no bearing on your problem and can actually confuse your mindset.

Take New Year's Eve, the night when we traditionally make resolutions to change our lives for the better. It's the most popular time for people to try to quit; it also happens to have the lowest success rate. By the end of the holidays, you've probably done more drinking than usual. You're sick of it, and you vow to quit as you're singing Auld Lang Syne at midnight.

After a few days, your motivation has waned somewhat. You're feeling cleansed and better about yourself, but the Little Monster is screaming for its fix. It couldn't hurt to have just one drink, could it? We all know how this ends.

Waiting for a "special" occasion is just another excuse for putting it off. Why would you want to put off your escape from the trap? The longer you stay in there, the worse it gets. You've been given the key—go now! If you happen to be reading this on New Year's Eve or any other special day, don't worry... you will get free in spite of that rather than because of it.

Think of everything you have to gain. A life free from slavery, dishonesty, misery, anger, deceit, self-loathing, helplessness. No more wasting your money on booze; no more covering up; no more worrying about your health; no more missing out on genuine pleasures; no more wanting to stop but feeling powerless to resist. Those days are gone.

Now you can look forward to living in the light, with your head held high, enjoying open, honest relationships with the people around you, feeling in control of how you spend your time and money, rediscovering the genuine pleasures you enjoyed before you became an emotional drinker.

With so much happiness to gain and so much misery to lose, what possible argument is there for waiting? It's time for the sixth instruction:

SIXTH INSTRUCTION: DON'T WAIT FOR THE RIGHT TIME TO QUIT. DO IT NOW!

If you understand the nature of the trap, are no longer plagued with doubts, and are eager to walk free, there's no reason to delay. If you're hesitating, please go through the RATIONALIZED list again.

YOUR FINAL DRINK

You may have already had what you regard as your final drink. Some people reach absolute certainty that they will never drink again long before this point. If that's you, don't worry; I'm not about to force you to drink! However, it is important that you go through this ritual and make a solemn vow.

You've made one of the most important decisions of your life. You're achieving something that all drinkers would love to achieve and that everybody, drinkers and non-drinkers alike, will admire you for. You're about to go up in the estimation of one person in particular: yourself.

Over time, as you become accustomed to the happy life of a non-drinker, all the motivation and determination you feel now will naturally fade. The ritual of the final drink provides you with a definitive moment that you can look back on, and it will remind you of everything you're feeling now. This is important, because it protects you from falling into the trap of thinking, "Well, I've proved I can control my drinking; surely one little drink won't hurt." You know that just one drink is all it takes to drag you back into the trap, so let's make sure you never forget that.

The thing that makes quitting hard with other methods is the lack of certainty, the eternal waiting to become a non-drinker. With Easyway you get certainty right away. There is nothing to wait for. You become a non-drinker the moment you finish your final drink, and you confirm your commitment to become a non-drinker when you make your vow. The ritual enables you to know when that moment is, to make that vow with a feeling of real intent, to visualize your victory over the two monsters and be able to say, "Yes! I'm a non-drinker now. I'm FREE!"

If you haven't already stopped drinking, pour your final drink now. If you have already had your final drink, think about that drink here.

Get comfortable, relax, and close your eyes for about 10 seconds. Focus on how the alcohol smells and the taste it leaves in your mouth as you drink it. Ask yourself if the misery it has caused you was worth it. Be aware that any feeling of pleasure or comfort is only relief at the Little Monster being calmed down for a while. Picture that monster and make a solemn vow to destroy it once and for all. Make that clear and certain decision a vow that you'll never drink alcohol again.

The ritual ends here. The vow marks the breaking of the cycle of addiction, in which each fix created the need or desire for the next. By breaking the cycle, you've removed the cause of the desire. You've drawn a boundary that you can always look back on as the moment you escaped your addiction to alcohol.

IN HER OWN WORDS: CARLY

"I don't think I've felt so certain of anything in my life as when I quit drinking. The clarity was incredible. I certainly hadn't expected to feel that when I started the book. I thought it might give me some tools to help me resist the temptation to drink, but it took away the temptation altogether.

"I look back now and wonder how I got into the state I was in. I turned to alcohol for just about anything: sadness, stress, boredom, loneliness, even celebration. That sounds funny—'even' celebration. The thing is, you don't feel like doing much celebrating when you're an alcoholic. It's the miserable feelings that seem to dominate.

"So when that door swings open and you realize you don't have any lingering desire for alcohol, it's like the sun bursting through the clouds. I remember the moment vividly because of the final drink ritual. I knew I'd had my final drink before I made my vow, so I didn't have another one—but the effect was just as powerful. I thought about that Little Monster and I felt a moment of revulsion, followed by a flash of joy as I realized I never had to put that stuff inside me again. I felt clean and free. It was like being reborn!

"I often go back to that moment now, eight years down the line, not because I need to but because I like to. It's a constant source of joy, and I give myself a pat on the back every time I go back there. Life is so good. It's probably no better than any non-drinker's life, but it feels better because I know what it feels like to live without that freedom and control.

"I'm so grateful to Easyway. It literally gave me new life."

AND THAT'S IT! YOU'RE FREE!

Now that you've made your vow, you can keep enjoying life as a non-drinker. Imagine you've just arrived at a beautiful vacation home with a lovely pool. You can take time to get used to your surroundings, or you can dive right in. The choice is yours. You might want to reflect on what you've achieved for a while, but there is absolutely nothing to wait for.

Carly talks about giving herself a pat on the back—you should too! You deserve it. Rejoice. Be proud. You've achieved something wonderful. And it's not going to end. You don't have to watch over it for the rest of your life. You're free, and that means you can keep living life, and enjoying it.

Chapter 18

GET ON WITH ENJOYING LIFE

IN THIS CHAPTER
•*RESPONDING TO WITHDRAWAL* •*THE LOBSTER TANK*
•*BAD DAYS* •*"JUST ONE DRINK"* •*REDISCOVER*
GENUINE PLEASURES •*THE LAST WORD*

Congratulations! What you've achieved is wonderful. All we need to do is make sure that the success you're enjoying now stays with you for the rest of your life.

It's important to ensure that, having escaped from the trap, you never fall or get dragged back in. It's time for the final instruction:

SEVENTH INSTRUCTION: ONCE YOU'VE STOPPED, NEVER DRINK AGAIN.

For a few days after your final drink, you may still feel the Little Monster crying out as it goes through its death throes. This can trigger a range of reactions, and you need to be ready for them. It's important that you don't ignore the feeling—but you shouldn't fear it either. As long as you have the right mindset, they won't be any problem at all. This is the "dreaded" withdrawal period that's said to be such an ordeal, especially by people who have tried to quit with the willpower method. In truth, for them it often is an ordeal, because they respond to the Little Monster's death throes in the wrong way. They think, "I need a drink." They know they don't want to drink, so this response triggers a mental struggle, and that anxiety causes the physical symptoms associated with withdrawal. It's the mental struggle that makes it hard.

WITHOUT THE MENTAL STRUGGLE, THE WITHDRAWAL PERIOD IS NO PROBLEM.

At worst, living with the Little Monster's death throes is no harder than having the flu for a few days. For most people, the physical symptoms are nowhere near as severe as the flu. They only become a problem if you let them sow a seed of doubt in your mind, or interpret them as a need or desire to drink.

If you do feel withdrawal symptoms, picture a Little Monster searching around the desert for a drink and you having control of the supply. You want that monster to die. All you have to do is keep the supply line closed. It's as easy as that.

You can control your mental response. Instead of thinking, "I need a drink, but I'm not allowed to have one," think, "This is the Little Monster demanding its fix. This is what emotional drinkers suffer from all their addicted lives. Happy non-drinkers don't suffer from this. Isn't that great? I'm a happy non-drinker and am free of it forever." Simply by rewiring your brain in this way, you will turn those withdrawal pangs into moments of pleasure.

Remember the power of your senses. Focus on what you feel and allow yourself to become aware that there is no physical pain—the only discomfort you might be feeling is not because you've stopped drinking, but because you started in the first place. Remind yourself that if you were to try to stop the feeling by drinking alcohol again, you would ensure suffering it for the rest of your life.

Take pleasure in starving that Little Monster. Revel in its suffering. Feel no guilt about rejoicing in its death.

WHY QUITTERS FAIL: THE LOBSTER TANK

As you continue to arm yourself for life free from drinking, it's useful to understand the main reasons why people do get hooked again.

The first is the influence of drinkers. The reason a lobster tank doesn't have a lid is that if a lobster tries to escape, the others drag it back down. Drinkers are very much the same. They don't like to see other drinkers escape because it compounds their feelings of slavery and fear.

If a drinker tries to drag you back in, remind yourself that they are behaving like that out of fear, which was created by the drug, and that you're incredibly lucky to have escaped from that nightmare. Just smile and tell them how great it is to be free. You might inspire them to quit themselves.

What is important is that you never envy drinkers. Pity them, by all means—they are all flies at different stages of their descent into the pitcher plant, and they don't realize the nectar is an illusion. But resist the urge to preach, particularly when they've had a drink or two. When they realize you're having a good time without booze, they'll start to ask questions. Then you'll be dealing with a more open-minded audience, but proceed with caution. When you're free, it's great to see another drinker escape, but trying to force them to see the error of their ways is like trying to force a claustrophobic into a lift.

WHY QUITTERS FAIL: BAD DAYS

The second trigger for failure is using a bad day as an excuse to drink. Of course, there will be days when you find it hard to see the joy in life. That's normal. Everybody has days when everything that can go wrong does go wrong. It has nothing to do with the fact that you've stopped drinking. The fact is when you're not a slave to alcohol, the bad days don't come around so often.

For people who quit with the willpower method, bad days can take them right back to emotional drinking. Without understanding about the brainwashing and the trap, they will interpret normal feelings of stress, irritability, or sometimes even hunger as "I need a drink," long after the physical withdrawal has ended. They'll resist the urge, though, because they've made a huge effort to quit. Instead they'll feel deprived, and that will make the stress and irritability worse.

Eventually their willpower will give out and they'll "treat themselves." They'll promise themselves it's "just one," but soon they'll find themselves hooked again. If their willpower doesn't give out, they'll spend the rest of their lives enduring the agony of wondering when the sense of deprivation will end.

You might find that when you have bad days, the thought of drinking comes into your mind, even though you've killed the Big Monster and you're convinced that you have no desire to drink again. Don't worry about this, but don't try to blot it out, either. Remember, you cannot tell your brain to *not* think about something. If you try to stop yourself from thinking about drinking, you'll get frustrated and miserable.

Accept that thoughts of drinking will cross your mind from time to time. They don't have to be a threat. When you have no desire to drink, you can think about drinking all you want, just as you can think about arsenic all you want without feeling compelled to take it. Better still, you can use the situation to remind yourself of the wonderful truth. Instead of telling yourself, "I can't drink," as someone who quits with the willpower method would, tell yourself, "Yippee! I'm free!"

The fourth instruction was never to doubt or question your decision to quit. This is essential. If you allow doubt to creep into your mind, you'll allow the Big Monster back in, and soon you'll be dragged back into the trap. Prepare yourself for the bad days and have your mindset ready. Protect yourself against getting caught out by it. Be ready for feelings of stress, irritability, sadness, loneliness, disappointment, or apathy, and remind yourself that you are better equipped to handle them now than when you were an emotional drinker. Drinking only makes it worse.

WHY QUITTERS FAIL: "JUST ONE DRINK"

The third reason for failure is the fallacy of "just one drink." People find that our claim is true; they have quit easily and painlessly, and they think that means they can have "just one drink" and then stop again just as easily. But the alcohol trap doesn't work like that, does it? "Just one drink" will create a new Little Monster that will demand another, and another, and another. Anyway, either you've killed the Big Monster or you haven't. If you believe there's value in having one drink, you'll believe it's worth having a million.

Whatever your reason is for picking up this book and committing to breaking free, something triggered that decision. In that respect, you are one of the lucky ones. Most emotional drinkers never get a trigger—or if they do, they are too inebriated to respond. So seize this opportunity you have given yourself with both hands, and always cherish your freedom.

If you think you can have "just one drink," you will get dragged back into the trap, and another trigger may never come along. How long did it take you to get here? How many years have passed since your first-ever drink? You could be looking at a lifetime of slavery.

REDISCOVER GENUINE PLEASURES

You are now in the so-called withdrawal period. Not so bad, is it? One of the great benefits of breaking free from emotional drinking with Easyway is that it not only helps you break free without a struggle, it also frees you immediately. You don't have to wait for the Little Monster to die before you start enjoying life again.

Freedom began the moment you finished your Final Drink and made your vow.

NOW IT'S TIME TO GET ON WITH LIFE.

Enjoy the springboard effect. On the one hand, you're freeing yourself from slavery; on the other, you're about to rediscover life's genuine pleasures. It's a win-win.

Like all addictions, emotional drinking takes away the ability to enjoy the things that you used to enjoy. Everything from reading books to watching movies, partying, exercising, and having sex loses its appeal. It's a consequence of the effect the drug has on your brain, hijacking the pleasure pathways and building up such a tolerance to the bombardment of chemicals that genuine pleasures no longer register.

Every addict knows that feeling of joylessness, where nothing can make you happy. They turn to their drug in the hope that it will lift their mood but, of course, it has the opposite effect. Now that you're a happy non-drinker, you can enjoy the sensation of your pleasure pathways becoming responsive again and rediscovering genuine pleasures to get excited about again.

You'll be amazed that situations you considered dull or even irritating become stimulating and enjoyable again: simple pleasures like spending time with your loved ones, going for walks, and seeing friends. Even work—which many addicts find hard to hold down because they find it so hard to motivate themselves—will become more enjoyable and rewarding, as you discover that your concentration, creativity, and ability to handle stress are so much better.

You'll rediscover the pleasure of meals, which become an irritating sideshow for many addicts. Your taste buds will come back to life, meaning you savor your food and start enjoying more nutritious meals, rather than filling yourself with carbs just to line your stomach. This, in turn, will have a beneficial effect on your overall health, helping you feel more satisfied, energetic, and happy.

You'll start to appreciate the social side of eating, too. Dining is an opportunity to chat and relax. Emotional drinkers forgo this pleasure, because they're in such a hurry to get to their next drink.

Most importantly, you'll start to enjoy your own company again. You'll rediscover your self-respect, and that will make you more content with yourself. Time in your own company won't be time spent with a devious, deceitful, scared, miserable, self-loathing slave; it will be time spent with a bold, decisive, open, upbeat, self-respecting hero. You will be excited by your newfound sense of control. You will regularly want to pat yourself on the back—and rightly so.

YOU ARE FREE!

THE LAST WORD

You picked up this book in the hope that it would help you control your emotional drinking. While that is the happy outcome of Easyway, from the start there has been one objective behind everything I've said. That objective is the real aim of what we set out to achieve. It is not just to help you stop drinking, but to repair your mindset, to restore the logic that addiction drives out, so that whenever you think about the subject of alcohol, whether it's today or 20 years from now, you don't think "I need a drink!" but

"YES! I DON'T NEED TO DRINK ANY MORE. I'M FREE!"

The simple steps to achieving this mindset are to realize that there are no genuine benefits to drinking alcohol, that there is no real difference between the drinker you were and so-called "normal" drinkers (you just went deeper into the same trap), and that you've already escaped from the alcohol prison.

Enjoy your freedom!

Chapter 19

USEFUL REMINDERS

From time to time, you may find it helpful to remind yourself of some of the issues we've discussed. This final chapter is a summary of the key points, and a reminder of the instructions. You can refer to these any time you like, and they will help you remain a happy non-drinker for the rest of your life.

If you've turned straight to this page in the hope that you will find the solution to your emotional drinking problem, I'm afraid it won't work. You need to start from the beginning and read the entire book in order. Once you've done that, the information on this page will make perfect sense.

- **Don't wait for anything.** You are free from the moment you unravel the brainwashing and kill the Big Monster, and you can keep living life as a happy non-drinker as soon as you complete the ritual of the final drink and take that vow. You've cut off the supply to the Little Monster and unlocked the door of your prison.

- **If you don't think you've felt the moment of revelation, don't worry or try to force it.** It usually comes after an occasion when you previously would have drunk alcohol. You suddenly realize that the thought that you no longer drink didn't even cross your mind. Just keep enjoying your life, and it'll come along soon enough.

- **Be aware that a very important change is happening in your life.** You're making fantastic progress in terms of health, peace of mind, confidence, self-respect, money, freedom... and you're giving up absolutely nothing. You're not making any sacrifice whatsoever, because alcohol did nothing for you at all. It's a massive win-win. So approach every day with excitement and elation that the whole nightmare is finally over.

- **Share your achievement with those who are close to you if you wish.** You will feel an enormous relief when you come clean with everyone who has been affected by your emotional drinking and let them join in your elation at breaking free.

- **Keep in mind that any big change can involve a period of adjustment**, even when the change is definitely for the better. It can take time for your mind and body to adjust. If you experience any discomfort, or feel disoriented over the next few days, remind yourself that it's not because you stopped drinking, it's because you started in the first place. It'll go away soon. It's all part of the wonderful achievement of breaking free.

- **Never doubt or question your decision to stop—you know it's the right one.** It's the most important decision you'll ever make. If the thought enters your mind that life will be less enjoyable without alcohol, just remember how miserable it felt to be in the grip of the Big Monster. If you allow temptation to creep in, you will put yourself in an impossible position: miserable if you don't, and even more miserable if you do.

- **Accept that there will always be good days and bad days,** but remember that you will be stronger both physically and mentally without alcohol in your life, so you'll enjoy the good times more and handle the bad times better.

- **Forget using substitutes to help you through the withdrawal period.** You will just be perpetuating the myth that quitting is hard. You don't need any kind of substitute—and they don't work anyway.

- **Avoid alcohol-free imitations of alcoholic drinks, such as non-alcoholic wine and beer.** Like any other substitute, they perpetuate the illusion that you're missing out on something. It's only because of addiction to the drug that we think we like the taste. Alcohol-free alternatives cut out the drug and leave just the awful taste! Now that you'll be consuming drinks that quench rather than create thirst, you won't need to have a glass in your hand all the time, any more than you'll need a plate of food in your hand all evening. You'll feel more confident without it.

- **Avoid other drugs.** If alcohol didn't make you happy, why should any other drug? If you're tempted to try a so-called "recreational" substance, ask yourself why you would want to start the nightmare all over again. You know how the trap works. If you could talk to the innocent child you were all those years ago when you first dabbled in alcohol, what would you say, knowing what you know now? Don't you owe it to yourself to be completely free? If you are ever concerned about any other drug, get in touch with us via www.AllenCarr.com.

- **Remember: you've stopped drinking; you haven't stopped living.** You can now start enjoying life to the full. There's no need to change other aspects of your lifestyle, unless you want to anyway. If the only reason you used to go to bars was to drink, why go now? What would be the point? But if you want to spend time with good friends at a bar, then go. Why should you deprive yourself of their company just because they drink? Do vegetarians have to stay out of restaurants that serve meat? Enjoy breaking these associations between certain places and alcohol. If they're fun places to go regardless of alcohol, focus on the reasons why. If they're not, why go?

- **There is no need to avoid drinkers, nor to envy them.** Go out and enjoy social situations, and show yourself you can handle them without feeling tempted to drink. When you're with drinkers, remember that you're not being deprived—they are. They will be envying you because they will be wishing they could be free, like you.

- **If people ask why you're not drinking, you don't have to give them your life story.** Just say, "I don't drink." Why should you have to defend not taking a drug?

- **If you find yourself thinking, "I can never have another drink,"** try facing up to the only alternative: to have to spend the rest of your life pouring an endless stream of revolting, addictive poison down your throat. Change your focus: think how great it will feel never to have another hangover as long as you live.

- **If the thought of "just one drink" enters your mind**, make sure you respond with the thought, "Yes! I no longer have any desire to do that. I'm a happy non-drinker." The thought will pass very quickly, and your brain will quickly learn not to think it again.

- **Avoid trying to banish the thought of alcohol from your mind.** All that does is put alcohol front and center. Let's face it, the subject of alcohol will occasionally come up in conversation, or enter your mind for some reason, and over the next few days you might think about it a lot. That's not a problem. It's what you're thinking that counts. As long as you're ready to respond by thinking "Great! I'm free!" you'll be happy to think about booze.

- **Accept that your mind can misbehave.** At any point in the future, you might suddenly have the thought or feeling, "I want a drink." That's all it is: a thought or feeling. It will pass. It might be normal thirst, or it might just be that you've forgotten you quit. You have a choice. You can say, "I must not have a drink," and make yourself miserable; or you can say, "This is just a thought. Isn't it wonderful I don't have to act on it?"

- **If you do take a sip by mistake, there's no need to panic.** This can easily happen; for example, if you're drinking orange juice and someone else at the table is drinking vodka and orange juice. Just make a mental note to be more careful in future, and then forget about it. This doesn't mean you can get away with the occasional sip, though. You should, of course, do everything you can to avoid consuming alcohol, but if you do make a mistake, recognize it and move on.

- **Watch out for hidden alcohol,** for example in mouthwash or cough syrup. Try to avoid it. You can almost always find a non-alcoholic alternative. If you go to church where they take Communion, find out whether your church uses non-alcoholic wine. Some do. In this case it would be all right, because it's not a substitute for a desire for booze. If the wine is alcoholic, I would avoid it. You can take part in the ceremony in other ways. Foods cooked with alcohol are usually OK, because the alcohol normally evaporates. Steer clear of any foods where the alcohol is still "live," such as brandy butter and trifle.

- **Finally, if you ever dream that you're drinking again, don't lose sleep over it.** This is quite a common occurrence. It's also common for people who have been tortured in prison to dream that they're back in that situation. That doesn't mean they want to be. See the whole business of consuming alcohol for what it is: a horrible nightmare from which you've finally awoken for good.

- **Don't forget—everyone at Allen Carr's Easyway is happy to provide you with free advice in the event you have any concerns or queries.** Contact us via www. AllenCarr.com or join the Allen Carr's Easyway to Stop Drinking Alcohol Facebook Group.

THE INSTRUCTIONS

1. Follow all the instructions in order.

2. Keep an open mind.

3. Start with a feeling of elation.

4. Never doubt your decision to quit.

5. Ignore all advice and influences that conflict with Easyway.

6. Don't wait for the right time to quit. Do it now!

7. Once you've stopped, never drink again.

ALLEN CARR'S EASYWAY CENTERS

The following list indicates the countries where Allen Carr's Easyway To Stop Smoking Centers are currently operational.

Check www.AllenCarr.com for latest additions to this list.

The success rate at the centers, based on the three-month money-back guarantee, is over 90 percent.

Selected centers also offer sessions that deal with alcohol, other drugs, and weight issues. Please check with your nearest center, listed on the following pages, for details.

Allen Carr's Easyway guarantee that you will find it easy to stop at the centers or your money back.

JOIN US!

Allen Carr's Easyway Centers have spread throughout the world with incredible speed and success. Our global franchise network now covers more than 150 cities in over 45 countries. This amazing growth has been achieved entirely organically. Former addicts, just like you, were so impressed by the ease with which they stopped that they felt inspired to contact us to see how they could bring the method to their region.

If you feel the same, contact us for details on how to become an Allen Carr's Easyway To Stop Smoking or an Allen Carr's Easyway To Stop Drinking franchisee.

Email us at: join-us@allencarr.com including your full name, postal address, and region of interest.

SUPPORT US!

No, don't send us money!

You have achieved something really wonderful. Every time we hear of someone escaping from the sinking ship, we get a feeling of enormous satisfaction.

It would give us great pleasure to hear that you have freed yourself from the slavery of addiction, so please visit the following web page where you can tell us of your success, inspire others to follow in your footsteps, and hear about ways you can help to spread the word.

 www.allencarr.com/fanzone

You can "like" our Facebook page here **www.facebook.com/ AllenCarr**

Together, we can help further Allen Carr's mission: to cure the world of addiction.

ALLEN CARR'S EASYWAY CENTERS

LONDON CLINIC AND WORLDWIDE HEAD OFFICE
Park House, 14 Pepys Road, Raynes Park, London SW20 8NH
Tel: +44 (0)20 8944 7761
Fax: +44 (0)20 8944 8619
Email: mail@allencarr.com
Website: www.allencarr.com
Therapists: John Dicey, Colleen Dwyer, Crispin Hay, Emma Hudson, Rob Fielding, Sam Kelser, Rob Groves, Debbie Brewer-West, Mark Keen, Duncan Bhaskaran-Brown, Mark Newman, Gerry Williams (Alcohol), Monique Douglas (Weight)

WORLDWIDE PRESS OFFICE
Tel: +44 (0)7970 88 44 52
Contact: John Dicey
Tel: +44 (0)7970 88 44 52
Email: media@allencarr.com

NORTH AMERICAN CENTERS

U.S.A.
Sessions held throughout the USA
Tel: +1 855 440 3777
Email: support@usa.allencarr.com
Website: www.allencarr.com

New York
Tel: +1 855 440 3777
Therapists: Natalie Clays and Team
Email: support@usa.allencarr.com
Website: www.allencarr.com

Los Angeles
Tel: +1 855 440 3777
Therapists: Natalie Clays and Team
Email: support@usa.allencarr.com
Website: www.allencarr.com

Milwaukee (and South Wisconsin)
Tel: +1 262 770 1260
Therapist: Wayne Spaulding
Email: wayne@easywaywisconsin.com
Website: www.allencarr.com

CANADA
Tel: +1 855 440 3777
Therapist: Natalie Clays
Email: natalie@ca.allencarr.com
Website: www.allencarr.com

U.K. CENTERS

UK Clinic Information and Central Booking Line

Tel: 0800 389 2115 (UK only)

Birmingham

Tel & Fax: 0800 389 2115
Therapists: John Dicey, Colleen Dwyer, Crispin Hay, Emma Hudson, Rob Fielding, Sam Kelser, Rob Groves, Debbie Brewer-West, Mark Keen, Duncan Bhaskaran-Brown, Mark Newman
Email: mail@allencarr.com
Website: www.allencarr.com

Bournemouth

Tel: 0800 389 2115
Therapists: John Dicey, Colleen Dwyer, Crispin Hay, Emma Hudson, Rob Fielding, Sam Kelser, Rob Groves, Debbie Brewer-West, Mark Keen, Duncan Bhaskaran-Brown, Mark Newman
Email: mail@allencarr.com
Website: www.allencarr.com

Brentwood

Tel: 0800 389 2115
Therapists: John Dicey, Colleen Dwyer, Crispin Hay, Emma Hudson, Rob Fielding, Sam Kelser, Rob Groves, Debbie Brewer-West, Mark Keen, Duncan Bhaskaran-Brown, Mark Newman
Email: mail@allencarr.com
Website: www.allencarr.com

Brighton

Tel: 0800 389 2115
Therapists: John Dicey, Colleen Dwyer, Crispin Hay, Emma Hudson, Rob Fielding, Sam Kelser, Rob Groves, Debbie Brewer-West, Mark Keen, Duncan Bhaskaran-Brown, Mark Newman
Email: mail@allencarr.com
Website: www.allencarr.com

Bristol

Tel: 0800 389 2115
Therapists: John Dicey, Colleen Dwyer, Crispin Hay, Emma Hudson, Rob Fielding, Sam Kelser, Rob Groves, Debbie Brewer-West, Mark Keen, Duncan Bhaskaran-Brown, Mark Newman
Email: mail@allencarr.com
Website: www.allencarr.com

Cambridge

Tel: 0800 389 2115
Therapists: John Dicey, Colleen Dwyer, Crispin Hay, Emma Hudson, Rob Fielding, Sam Kelser, Rob Groves, Debbie Brewer-West, Mark Keen, Duncan Bhaskaran-Brown, Mark Newman
Email: mail@allencarr.com
Website: www.allencarr.com

Coventry

Tel: 0800 321 3007
Therapist: Rob Fielding
Email:
info@easywaymidlands.co.uk
Website: www.allencarr.com

Cumbria

Tel: 0800 389 2115
Therapists: John Dicey, Colleen
Dwyer, Crispin Hay, Emma
Hudson, Rob Fielding, Sam Kelser,
Rob Groves, Debbie Brewer-West,
Mark Keen, Duncan Bhaskaran-
Brown, Mark Newman
Email: mail@allencarr.com
Website: www.allencarr.com

Derby

Tel: 0800 389 2115
Therapists: John Dicey, Colleen
Dwyer, Crispin Hay, Emma
Hudson, Rob Fielding, Sam Kelser,
Rob Groves, Debbie Brewer-West,
Mark Keen, Duncan Bhaskaran-
Brown, Mark Newman
Email: mail@allencarr.com
Website: www.allencarr.com

Guernsey

Tel: 0800 077 6187
Therapist: Mark Keen
Email:
mark@easywaymanchester.co.uk
Website: www.allencarr.com

Isle of Man

Tel: 0800 077 6187
Therapist: Mark Keen
Email: mark@easywaymanchester.
co.uk
Website: www.allencarr.com

Jersey

Tel: 0800 077 6187
Therapist: Mark Keen
Email:
mark@easywaymanchester.co.uk
Website: www.allencarr.com

Kent

Tel: 0800 389 2115
Therapists: John Dicey, Colleen
Dwyer, Crispin Hay, Emma
Hudson, Rob Fielding, Sam Kelser,
Rob Groves, Debbie Brewer-West,
Mark Keen, Duncan Bhaskaran-
Brown, Mark Newman
Email: mail@allencarr.com
Website: www.allencarr.com

Lancashire

Tel: 0800 389 2115
Therapists: John Dicey, Colleen
Dwyer, Crispin Hay, Emma
Hudson, Rob Fielding, Sam Kelser,
Rob Groves, Debbie Brewer-West,
Mark Keen, Duncan Bhaskaran-
Brown, Mark Newman
Email: mail@allencarr.com
Website: www.allencarr.com

Leeds

Tel: 0800 077 6187
Therapist: Mark Keen
Email:
mark@easywaymanchester.co.uk
Website: www.allencarr.com

Leicester

Tel: 0800 321 3007
Therapist: Rob Fielding
Email:
info@easywaymidlands.co.uk
Website: www.allencarr.com

Lincoln

Tel: 0800 321 3007
Therapist: Rob Fielding
Email:
info@easywaymidlands.co.uk
Website: www.allencarr.com

Liverpool

Tel: 0800 389 2115
Therapists: John Dicey, Colleen Dwyer, Crispin Hay, Emma Hudson, Rob Fielding, Sam Kelser, Rob Groves, Debbie Brewer-West, Mark Keen, Duncan Bhaskaran-Brown, Mark Newman
Email: mail@allencarr.com
Website: www.allencarr.com

Manchester

Tel: 0800 077 6187
Therapist: Mark Keen
Email: mark@easywaymanchester.co.uk
Website: www.allencarr.com

Milton Keynes

Tel: 0800 389 2115
Therapists: John Dicey, Colleen Dwyer, Crispin Hay, Emma Hudson, Rob Fielding, Sam Kelser, Rob Groves, Debbie Brewer-West, Mark Keen, Duncan Bhaskaran-Brown, Mark Newman
Email: mail@allencarr.com
Website: www.allencarr.com

Newcastle/North East

Tel: 0800 389 2115
Therapists: John Dicey, Colleen Dwyer, Crispin Hay, Emma Hudson, Rob Fielding, Sam Kelser, Rob Groves, Debbie Brewer-West, Mark Keen, Duncan Bhaskaran-Brown, Mark Newman
Email: mail@allencarr.com
Website: www.allencarr.com

Nottingham

Tel: 0800 389 2115
Therapists:John Dicey, Colleen Dwyer, Crispin Hay, Emma Hudson, Rob Fielding, Sam Kelser, Rob Groves, Debbie Brewer-West, Mark Keen, Duncan Bhaskaran-Brown, Mark Newman
Email: mail@allencarr.com
Website: www.allencarr.com

Oxford

Tel: 0800 389 2115
Therapists: John Dicey, Colleen Dwyer, Crispin Hay, Emma Hudson, Rob Fielding, Sam Kelser, Rob Groves, Debbie Brewer-West, Mark Keen, Duncan Bhaskaran-Brown, Mark Newman
Email: mail@allencarr.com
Website: www.allencarr.com

Reading

Tel: 0800 389 2115
Therapists: John Dicey, Colleen Dwyer, Crispin Hay, Emma Hudson, Rob Fielding, Sam Kelser, Rob Groves, Debbie Brewer-West, Mark Keen, Duncan Bhaskaran-Brown, Mark Newman
Email: mail@allencarr.com
Website: www.allencarr.com

SCOTLAND
Glasgow and Edinburgh

Tel: +44 (0)131 449 7858
Therapists: Paul Melvin and Jim McCreadie
Email: info@easywayscotland.co.uk
Website: www.allencarr.com

Southampton

Tel: 0800 389 2115
Therapists: John Dicey, Colleen
Dwyer, Crispin Hay, Emma
Hudson, Rob Fielding, Sam Kelser,
Rob Groves, Debbie Brewer-West,
Mark Keen, Duncan Bhaskaran-
Brown, Mark Newman
Email: mail@allencarr.com
Website: www.allencarr.com

Southport

Tel: 0800 389 2115
Therapists: John Dicey, Colleen
Dwyer, Crispin Hay, Emma
Hudson, Rob Fielding, Sam Kelser,
Rob Groves, Debbie Brewer-West,
Mark Keen, Duncan Bhaskaran-
Brown, Mark Newman
Email: mail@allencarr.com
Website: www.allencarr.com

Staines/Heathrow

Tel: 0800 389 2115
Therapists: John Dicey, Colleen
Dwyer, Crispin Hay, Emma
Hudson, Rob Fielding, Sam Kelser,
Rob Groves, Debbie Brewer-West,
Mark Keen, Duncan Bhaskaran-
Brown, Mark Newman
Email: mail@allencarr.com
Website: www.allencarr.com

Stevenage

Tel: 0800 389 2115
Therapists: John Dicey, Colleen
Dwyer, Crispin Hay, Emma
Hudson, Rob Fielding, Sam Kelser,
Rob Groves, Debbie Brewer-West,
Mark Keen, Duncan Bhaskaran-
Brown, Mark Newman
Email: mail@allencarr.com
Website: www.allencarr.com

Stoke

Tel: 0800 389 2115
Therapists: John Dicey, Colleen
Dwyer, Crispin Hay, Emma
Hudson, Rob Fielding, Sam Kelser,
Rob Groves, Debbie Brewer-West,
Mark Keen, Duncan Bhaskaran-
Brown, Mark Newman
Email: mail@allencarr.com
Website: www.allencarr.com

Surrey

Park House, 14 Pepys Road, Raynes
Park, London SW20 8NH
Tel: +44 (0)20 8944 7761
Fax: +44 (0)20 8944 8619
Therapists: John Dicey, Colleen
Dwyer, Crispin Hay, Emma
Hudson, Rob Fielding, Sam Kelser,
Rob Groves, Debbie Brewer-West,
Mark Keen, Duncan Bhaskaran-
Brown, Mark Newman
Gerry Williams (Alcohol), Monique
Douglas (Weight)
Email: mail@allencarr.com
Website: www.allencarr.com

Watford

Tel: 0800 389 2115
Therapists: John Dicey, Colleen Dwyer, Crispin Hay, Emma Hudson, Rob Fielding, Sam Kelser, Rob Groves, Debbie Brewer-West, Mark Keen, Duncan Bhaskaran-Brown, Mark Newman
Email: mail@allencarr.com
Website: www.allencarr.com

Worcester

Tel: 0800 321 3007
Therapist: Rob Fielding
Email: info@easywaymidlands.co.uk
Website: www.allencarr.com

WORLDWIDE CENTERS

AUSTRALIA
ACT, NSW, NT, QLD, VIC

Tel: 1300 848 028
Therapist: Natalie Clays and Team
Email: natalie@allencarr.com.au
Website: www.allencarr.com

South Australia

Tel: 1300 848 028
Therapist: Jaime Reed
Email: sa@allencarr.com.au
Website: www.allencarr.com

Western Australia

Tel: 1300 848 028
Therapist: Natalie Clays and Team
Email: natalie@allencarr.com.au
Website: www.allencarr.com

AUSTRIA

Sessions held throughout Austria
Freephone: 0800RAUCHEN (0800 7282436)
Tel: +43 (0)3512 44755
Therapists: Erich Kellermann and Team
Email: info@allen-carr.at
Website: www.allencarr.com

BELGIUM
Brussels

Tel: +32 (0)2 808 19 65
Therapist: Paula Rooduijn
Email: info@allencarr.be
Website: www.allencarr.com

BRAZIL

Therapist : Lilian Brunstein
Email: contato@easywayonline.com.br
Website: www.allencarr.com

BULGARIA

Tel: 0800 14104/+359 899 88 99 07
Therapist: Rumyana Kostadinova
Email: rk@nepushaveche.com
Website: www.allencarr.com

CHILE

Tel: +56 2 4744587
Therapist: Claudia Sarmiento
Email: contacto@allencarr.cl
Website: www.allencarr.com

CYPRUS

Tel: +357 25770611
Therapist: Andreas Damianou
Email: info@allencarr.com.cy
Website: www.allencarr.com

DENMARK

Sessions held throughout Denmark
Tel: +45 70267711
Therapist: Mette Fønss
Email: mette@easyway.dk
Website: www.allencarr.com

ESTONIA

Tel: +372 733 0044
Therapist: Henry Jakobson
Email: info@allencarr.ee
Website: www.allencarr.com

FINLAND

Tel: +358-(0)45 3544099
Therapist: Janne Ström
Email: info@allencarr.fi
Website: www.allencarr.com

FRANCE

Sessions held throughout France
Freephone: 0800 386387
Tel: +33 (4)91 33 54 55
Therapists: Erick Serre and Team
Email: info@allencarr.fr
Website: www.allencarr.com

GERMANY

Sessions held throughout Germany
Freephone: 08000RAUCHEN
(0800 07282436)
Tel: +49 (0)8031 90190-0
Therapists: Erich Kellermann
and Team
Email: info@allen-carr.de
Website: www.allencarr.com

GREECE

Sessions held throughout Greece
Tel: +30 210 5224087
Therapist: Panos Tzouras
Email: panos@allencarr.gr
Website: www.allencarr.com

GUATEMALA

Tel: +502 2362 0000
Therapist: Michelle Binford
Email:
info@dejadefumarfacil.com
Website: www.allencarr.com

HONG KONG

Email: info@easywayhongkong.com
Website: www.allencarr.com

HUNGARY

Seminars in Budapest and
12 other cities across Hungary
Tel: 06 80 624 426 (freephone) or
+36 20 580 9244
Therapist: Gábor Szász
Email: szasz.gabor@allencarr.hu
Website: www.allencarr.com

INDIA
Bangalore and Chennai

Tel: +91 (0)80 4154 0624
Therapist: Suresh Shottam
Email: info@
easywaytostopsmoking.co.in
Website: www.allencarr.com

IRAN

Please check website for details
Tehran and Mashhad
Website: www.allencarr.com

ISRAEL

Sessions held throughout Israel
Tel: +972 (0)3 6212525
Therapists: Orit Rozen and Team
Email: info@allencarr.co.il
Website: www.allencarr.com

ITALY

Sessions held throughout Italy
Tel/Fax: +39 (0)2 7060 2438
Therapists: Francesca Cesati and Team
Email: info@easywayitalia.com
Website: www.allencarr.com

JAPAN

Sessions held throughout Japan
www.allencarr.com

LEBANON

Tel: +961 1 791 5565
Therapist: Sadek El-Assaad
Email: info@AllenCarrEasyWay.me
Website: www.allencarr.com

MAURITIUS

Tel: +230 5727 5103
Therapist: Heidi Hoareau
Email: info@allencarr.mu
Website: www.allencarr.com

MEXICO

Sessions held throughout Mexico
Tel: +52 55 2623 0631
Therapists: Jorge Davo and Team
Email: info@allencarr-mexico.com
Website: www.allencarr.com

NETHERLANDS

Sessions held throughout the
Netherlands
Allen Carr's Easyway
'stoppen met roken'
Tel: +31 53 478 43 62/
+31 900 786 77 37
Email: info@allencarr.nl
Website: www.allencarr.com

NEW ZEALAND
North Island – Auckland

Tel: +64 (0) 800 848 028
Therapist: Natalie Clays and Team
Email: natalie@allencarr.co.nz
Website: www.allencarr.com

South Island – Wellington and Christchurch

Tel: +64 (0) 800 848 028
Therapist: Natalie Clays and Team
Email: natalie@allencarr.co.nz

NORWAY

Therapist: Laila Thorsen
Please check website for details
Website: www.allencarr.com

PERU
Lima

Tel: +511 637 7310
Therapist: Luis Loranca
Email: lloranca@
dejardefumaraltoque.com
Website: www.allencarr.com

POLAND

Sessions held throughout Poland
Tel: +48 (0)22 621 36 11
Therapist: Michael Spyrka
Email: info@allen-carr.pl
Website: www.allencarr.com

POLAND – Alcohol sessions

Tel: +48 71 307 32 37
Therapist: Maciej Kramarz
Email: mk@allen-carr.com.pl
Website: www.allencarr.com

PORTUGAL
Oporto
Tel: +351 22 9958698
Therapist: Ria Slof
Email:
info@comodeixardefumar.com
Website: www.allencarr.com

REPUBLIC OF IRELAND
Dublin
Tel: +353 (0)1 499 9010
Therapists: Paul Melvin & Jim
McCreadie
Email: info@allencarr.ie
Website: www.allencarr.com

ROMANIA
Tel: +40 (0)7321 3 8383
Therapist: Cristina Nichita
Email: raspunsuri@allencarr.ro
Website: www.allencarr.com

RUSSIA
Allen Carr's Easyway to Stop
Smoking
Live Seminars & Online Video
Programme
Tel: +7 495 644 64 26
Freecall +7 (800) 250 6622
Therapist: Alexander Fomin
Email: info@allencarr.ru
Website: www.allencarr.com

Allen Carr's Easyway to Stop
Drinking
Live Seminars & Online Video
Programme
Tel: +8 (800) 302 80 68
+7 985 207 47 93
Therapist: Artem Kasyanov
Email: info@allencarrlife.ru
Website: www.allencarr.com

St Petersburg
Please check website for details
Website: www.allencarr.com

SERBIA
Belgrade
Tel: +381 (0)11 308 8686
Email: office@allencarr.co.rs
Website: www.allencarr.com

SINGAPORE
Tel: +65 62241450
Therapist: Pam Oei
Email: pam@allencarr.com.sg
Website: www.allencarr.com

SLOVENIA
Tel: +386 (0)40 77 61 77
Therapist: Grega Sever
Email: easyway@easyway.si
Website: www.allencarr.com

SOUTH AFRICA
Sessions held throughout South
Africa
National Booking Line:
0861 100 200
Head Office: 15 Draper Square,
Draper St, Claremont 7708, Cape
Town
Cape Town: Dr Charles Nel
Tel: +27 (0)21 851 5883
Mobile: 083 600 5555
Therapists: Dr Charles Nel,
Malcolm Robinson and Team
Email: easyway@allencarr.co.za
Website: www.allencarr.com

SOUTH KOREA
Seoul
Tel: +82 (0)70 4227 1862
Therapist: Yousung Cha
Email: master@allencarr.co.kr
Website: www.allencarr.com

SPAIN
Tel: +34 910 05 29 99
Therapist: Luis Loranca
Email: informes@AllenCarrOfficial.es
Website: www.allencarr.com

SWEDEN
Tel: +46 70 695 6850
Therapists: Nina Ljungqvist,
Renée Johansson
Email: info@easyway.se
Website: www.allencarr.com

SWITZERLAND
Sessions held throughout
Switzerland
Freephone: 0800RAUCHEN
(0800/728 2436)
Tel: +41 (0)52 383 3773
Fax: +41 (0)52 383 3774
Therapists: Cyrill Argast and Team
For sessions in Suisse Romand
and Svizzera Italiana:
Tel: 0800 386 387
Email: info@allen-carr.ch
Website: www.allencarr.com

TURKEY
Sessions held throughout Turkey
Tel: +90 212 358 5307
Therapist: Emre Üstünuçar
Email: info@allencarr.com.tr
Website: www.allencarr.com

UNITED ARAB EMIRATES
Dubai and Abu Dhabi
Tel: +97 56 693 4000
Therapist: Sadek El-Assaad
Email: info@AllenCarrEasyWay.me
Website: www.allencarr.com

OTHER ALLEN CARR PUBLICATIONS

Allen Carr's revolutionary Easyway method is available in a wide variety of formats, including digitally as audiobooks and ebooks, and has been successfully applied to a broad range of subjects. For more information about Easyway publications, please visit

shop.allencarr.com

The Easy Way to Quit Smoking

The Easy Way to Quit Vaping

The Illustrated Easy Way to Stop Smoking

Allen Carr's Easy Way for Women to Quit Smoking

The Illustrated Easy Way for Women to Stop Smoking

Your Personal Stop Smoking Plan

Finally Free!

Smoking Sucks (Parent Guide with 16 page pull-out comic)

The Little Book of Quitting Smoking

How to Be a Happy Nonsmoker

No More Ashtrays

The Only Way to Stop Smoking Permanently

How to Stop Your Child Smoking

The Easy Way to Control Alcohol

Allen Carr's Quit Drinking Without Willpower

Your Personal Stop Drinking Plan

Allen Carr's Easy Way for Women to Quit Drinking

The Illustrated Easy Way to Stop Drinking

No More Hangovers

The Easy Way to Mindfulness

Smart Phone Dumb Phone

Good Sugar Bad Sugar

The Easy Way to Quit Sugar

The Easy Way to Lose Weight

Allen Carr's Easy Way for Women to Lose Weight

No More Diets

The Easy Way to Stop Gambling

No More Gambling

No More Worrying

Get Out of Debt Now

No More Debt

No More Fear of Flying

The Easy Way to Quit Caffeine

Packing It In The Easy Way
(the autobiography)

Easyway publications are also available as **audiobooks**.
Visit **shop.allencarr.com** to find out more.

DISCOUNT VOUCHER
for
ALLEN CARR'S
EASYWAY CENTERS

Recover the price of this book when you attend an
Allen Carr's Easyway Center
anywhere in the world!

Allen Carr's Easyway has a global network of stop
smoking centers where we guarantee you'll find it easy
to stop smoking or your money back.

**The success rate based on this
unique money-back guarantee is over 90%.**

Sessions addressing weight, alcohol, and other
drug addictions are also available at certain centers.

When you book your session, mention this
voucher and you'll receive a discount off
the price of this book. Contact your nearest
center for more information on how the sessions
work and to book your appointment.

**Details of Allen Carr's Easyway
Centers can be found at**
www.allencarr.com

This offer is not valid in conjunction with any other offer/promotion.